You need one small room for yourself.
That is very true.
When you find yourself really in the small room,
as one of your rooms,
then there is you yourself
and the whole universe is there.
The whole universe makes sense to you.
Without your room, the whole universe
does not make any sense.

—Suzuki-roshi

WRITTEN & ILLUSTRATED BY TOM SCHNEIDER

THE MOVEABLE NEST

A DELTA BOOK

A DELTA BOOK

Published by
Dell Publishing Co., Inc.
1 Dag Hammarskjold Plaza
New York, New York 10017

Delta ® TM 755118, Dell Publishing Co., Inc.

Printed in the United States of America

First printing—August 1981

ISBN: 0-440-56383-6

In memory of my dad, Ray "Pete" Schneider,
who taught me the fine art of tinkering.

And thanks (again) to my friends and colleagues:
Linda Allison, Gordon Ashby, J. Baldwin, Linda and Hal Bennett, Bill
Broder, Marilyn Burns, Jerry and Chris Celotti-Kay,
Rusty Dillon, Sue and Phil Frank, Martha Freebairn-
Smith, Gerald George, Gary Gutierrez, Jamie and
Marilyn Jobb, Lorinda Lumbert, Tom Mork, Mollie Rights,
Jim and Carolyn Robertson, Bonnie Laurie Russell,
Lee Sannella, Drew Takahashi, Deborah Todd, Chris
Trahan, Bill and Patty Wells, Richard Wilson,
Bill VanderVen, Marci Yellin.

For patience beyond the call:
Cynthia Vartan (my editor)
Edith Jordan Schneider (my mother)
Jordan Christopher Schneider (my son)

Contents

Cover walls   22
Comparing prices, ease of installation and removal, and portability of two dozen different wall coverings, including paint, fabric, shingles, cork, and other wood products.

Paint (Nothing else covers a wall for 2 cents a square foot.)   24
The fine art of filling holes. Selecting the right paint for your purposes. When not to use a roller. New painting tools – edgers, pads – how good are they?

On and Off the Wall   30
From paste-on picture hooks to heavy-duty toggle bolts... a working guide to some 20 wall fasteners. How to select the right fastener for each job. Some new uses for familiar fasteners. Special problems: like hanging a mirror on a brick wall.

Wall Dressing   46
Fabrics as wall coverings. How to put them up so you can take them down. Ready-made hangings. Cloth-wrapped cardboard "tiles."

Frame-Ups   50
With frames... decorative fabrics, bulletin boards, posters and prints... all go up quickly and come down easily. How to choose and use framable treasures to make a place your own.

4   Underfoot   101

Leases, Rental Agreements and The Moveable Nest

Not space here for a course in landlord/tenant law. (That's another book, or two) But here are the highlights, especially those parts of the law that may affect remodeling painting, wall fasteners, and other nest-building plans. I've included excerpts (unexpurgated) from my own lease.

Is It a Lease or a Leash?

Finding that balance: will your landlord/landlady leave you alone while you're building your fantasy, but still be around when the water heater springs a leak?

Deeper into the Lease

Understanding the wording in your lease or rental agreement. What are the _can's_, _can't's_, and _must's_ regarding maintenance and alterations.

Overdoing it Yourself

The make-your-own-repairs-and-deduct-it deal and some possible drawbacks.

Shopping Lists

Stalking the Yellow Pages

Unusual hardware is found in unlikely places: ship chandlers, music stores, restaurant suppliers, sporting goods stores, and more.

16

Introduction

Have it both ways: the flexibility of being able to pick up and move easily; the pleasure and security of a place that feels like home. *The Moveable Nest* will help you put energy into a unique, personal, affordable environment that's as changeable as you need it to be. Here is a positive approach to an increasingly common dilemma: how to get some of the benefits of home ownership, without the impossible burdens.

Overhead, underfoot, on and off the walls, in bite-size chunks, the elements of portable nest-building are carefully dissected. Costs are compared, hardware is described, solutions are offered. Then it's up to you. From the twenty different wall fasteners described and illustrated, you find the one that adapts to your needs. From an under-standing of the three basic kinds of lighting, you select an approach and fixtures that fit your space. It could be an off-the-shelf industrial lamp, or a bulb and shade hanging from a tree branch. The final effect will be yours to brag about, because the steps along the way—the design decisions—are all your own.

No full-color photos here. No stylish rooms to copy. *The Moveable Nest* is a down-to-earth source book of drawings, plans, and details. Think of it as a tool, and a prod; an invitation to unlock your own design sensibilities. You don't need to be a master carpenter to use it. You don't need an arsenal of tools. All you need is what you've already got: imagination—the willingness to change.

A detailed, illustrated book of designs that doesn't limit choices? It's all in how you look at it. *The Moveable Nest* is mostly modeled on *my* moveable nest. It's a conden-sation of my nineteen-year ex-perience of moving, making, collecting, and discarding parts and pieces of my porta-ble "home." I'd like to show you what has worked for me. You can take it literally, bor-row freely and duplicate it, or you can use it as inspiration— a takeoff point for your own ideas.

My own moveable nest is al-ways changing. I think of it as reusable cake batter. Each time I load the moving van, I stir in the latest ingredients. When unloaded at the new place, the mixture begins to rise and fill the space avail-able. In each new situation, some ingredients are added or subtracted until the recipe feels right.

When I move, the last items to be packed and the first to be unloaded are the workbench, shelves, and tools for my portable shop. (There's a photo of it, set up in my present place, on the back cover.) No project in this book is too big for that shop. But even a modest setup like mine is not a requirement. Each chapter begins with quick and simple solutions—the tools needed are scissors, stapler, hammer, tacks, glue, etc.—then moves on to projects that take more time and more equipment.

These larger projects assume some basic woodworking skills and some savvy with tools. If you can't do it all, you might hire some help with the heavier woodcutting. I've found some cabinetmakers are very willing to take on a piece of a project, and if asked, will usually contribute helpful suggestions. Get several referrals from lumber retailers, and then shop around for someone who feels friendly.

Keep in mind that tools are built to overpower wood and metal. They will do the same—with even greater dispatch—to pieces of your body. I've built nearly everything in the book, and I still have ten good fingers and toes. The projects were designed to be handsome, portable, and safe to use ... when complete. Your own process of getting from plans to finished item is something I can't guarantee. That part is up to you. Please work with full attention and care.

To enrich and thicken my own experience, I have blended in some ideas and insights from my friends, who are, by choice or necessity, involved in similar kinds of living experiments. J. Baldwin, soft tech and nomadics editor of *Co-Evolution Quarterly* and *The Next Whole Earth Catalog*, was my authority on energy-saving devices. Architect and designer Bill Wells was always there for ideas and knowledgeable critiques. Richard Wilson gave me monthly design seminars.

I've also had help from experts in the legal field. They seem to agree that you shouldn't make extensive changes in a place you don't own without some understanding of laws about leases and landlord-tenant relationships. So, even before you lift a paintbrush, you might want to look over "Leases, Rental Agreements, and The Moveable Nest" (p. 155). And while you're rummaging about in the back of the book, note that there is a glossary, "Shop Talk," to make sense out of the private language spoken only in hardware stores and lumberyards, as well as "Shopping Lists," to guide you toward bargains, unusual sources of materials, and the manufacturers of specific products mentioned in the text.

Incidentally, the use of a brand name (it will be in italics) means only that one manufacturer has a unique (perhaps patented) product, or that it is the most widely known, or that the product and/or information about it are available by mail.

That's what you get. Information, ideas, and encouragement. There are no warranties, expressed or implied. This book can only be an extension of your own head and hands. I've tried to design the most useful tool I could. And to make it comfortable and warm to the touch. Now, it's your move. 🐌

Here is a handy way to wear your tool kit. This is my own edited collection. It's remarkably complete for most small jobs.

My kit of wall fasteners for all occasions.

1
The
Wall

Richard is one of my most fastidious friends. This is his approach to moving into a new apartment: He unpacks almost nothing. Then for three, four, seven solid days—whatever it takes—he scrapes, sands, fills, and paints the new place, forcing it in one overbearingly intentional motion toward pure, white cleanliness. In going over every inch of the place he experiences two positive benefits. First, the apartment becomes *his.* From this day forward he knows that all the dirt will be new dirt, *his* dirt. But more importantly, he comes to really know every nook and cranny of the place, to see its possibilities. His fertile, spatially adept mind is thinking, planning, designing all the while he's painting. His liking for the place grows as he invests his physical energy and his imagination.

Paint does have this winning quality. It can put a new skin on the whole place in a modest amount of time with a modest amount of effort and expense. And let's face it. You *will* be depressed if you have to live even a few weeks with the previous tenant's idea of self-expression. You know what I mean: One apple-green "accent wall" in an otherwise lemon-yellow bedroom. Or shiny orange-enameled cabinets next to avocado-green appliances. Or pink semi-gloss woodwork rimming royal-purple walls.

But paint is no panacea. (If it were, most of this chapter would not be needed.) One reason paint isn't everything: Now that "landlord white" has replaced "landlord beige" as the standard rental-unit color, those of us who have white-washed dozens of rentals with

the fervor of religious zealots are experiencing a somewhat hollow victory. (Just as International Style architecture was more exciting when it was rising next to the excesses of the Romanesque and Gothic revivals.) Once the world has been won over to white (and to the International Style) it gets rather boring.

Some moderation, then, is in order. Live in the new place awhile. Paint out the pink and purple aberrations—and sit with the rest. Move in the furniture. Hang a bold cotton print on a bare wall. Look at the colors in these things that you like and see if they suggest a treatment for the walls. Just as white may not be the answer, so may not paint.

Think in different categories. Read on! 🐌

Coverwalls

Here is a list of traditional and out-of-the ordinary wall covering materials ranked by cost per square foot. Price is only one consideration, of course, but the list does serve up some surprises. For instance, I wouldn't have guessed that ceramic tile (made from clay, right?) would cost more than oak parquet. And I'm surprised but pleased to see that versatile, reusable denim runs only a penny more than wallpaper. The price used to determine square foot figures is provided, so you can make adjustments for your area (and inflation).

COST/ SQ. FT.	MATERIAL	PRICE AS SOLD	COMMENTS
.02	PAINT	@ 7.95/gallon Covers 400 sq.ft.	The least expensive wall covering, it's also decidedly not reusable. (See p. 24.)
.05	NATURAL BURLAP	@ .59/yard 40" wide	An old standby. Easily stapled in place. Looks good with wood battens. Changes color in sun.
.08	SPLIT BAMBOO	(Sold as fencing) @ 7.95/roll: 6 x 15 ft.	A bit too rustic for some interiors. Won't reach ceiling when used vertically.
.13	WALLPAPER (Prepasted)	@ 3.95/single roll Covers ± 30 sq.ft.	No wallpaper (yet) is reusable. Listed here for comparison. Cloth is a better investment.
.14	DENIM	@ 1.69/yard 48" wide	A tough, good-looking wall covering. Also good for drapes and upholstery. Fades in bright sun.
.15	ARTIST'S CANVAS (Unprimed)	@ 1.99/yard 52" wide	A moderately heavy weight cotton duck. Handsome off-white color. Staple to wall or to stretcher frames.
.19	INSULATION BOARD "Celotex", "TemJack", etc.	@ 6.00/ 4 x 8 ft sheet ½" thick	Cover an unused door or construct a temporary wall. Make an entire wall a bulletin board. Prepainted.
.21	CLOTH-BACKED VINYL	@ 2.79/yard 54" wide	Waterproof. Use with battens in bathroom. Also excellent for covering worktables. (See p. 113)
*A,B .22	LAUAN MAHOGANY STRIPS	@ 6.95/package Covers 32 sq.ft.	Least expensive real wood paneling. Too thin to nail. Must be glued to subpanel (Adds to cost.)
.23	ARTIST'S CANVAS (Primed)	@ 2.99/yard 52" wide	Water resistant. Staple to stretcher frames and paint your own graphic panels.

* A = Needs varnish or sealer for finish. (Not included in cost.)   B = Small units: For best portability, prenail pieces together across the back, or glue them to modular subpanels.

COST/ SQ. FT.	MATERIAL	PRICE AS SOLD	COMMENTS
.29	CORK TILES	@ .88 / package of 3 - 12"x 12" tiles	Lightweight. Some acoustic and heat insulating value. Useful as pinboard. Some object to odor.
.32 B	REDWOOD LATH	@ 7.95/bundle (50 pcs) 1½" x 48" covers 25 sq.ft.	Rough to the touch. Best left unfinished, or use sealer. Nice in bathrooms (but water splash will discolor).
.37 B	CEDAR SHINGLES (Rustic #4 Grade)	@ 9.49/bundle covers 25 sq.ft	Rough to the touch. Dust catcher. Leave unfinished, or use sealer. Direct water splash will stain.
.42 A, B	PECKY CEDAR	@ 9.95/package Covers 24 sq.ft	Random lengths. Holes (pecks?) will let whatever's underneath show through.
.47 A	KNOTTY PINE (Sometimes called "shelving")	1"x 12" (¾" x 11½" actual) @ .45 / lineal foot	Not tongue and groove. May need battens. If boards are butted together cracks may look bad.
.49	MIRROR TILE	@ .49 each (Tiles are 12"x 12")	Takes practice to cut special sizes. Best used on one wall as accent. Makes room look larger.
.59	NYLON CARPET (Foam backed - no pad needed)	@ 7.08 / lineal foot 12 feet wide on roll	Very low maintenance. Acoustic and heat insulating. Staple to wall or glue to subpanel. (see p 106)
.61 A, B	REDWOOD BENDER BOARD	⅜" x 3¾" actual width @ 19 / lineal foot	Rough to the touch. Looks best unfinished or use only sealer. Direct water splash will stain.
.95	PINE PANELING (White Pine)	@ 21.95/package Covers 23 sq.ft.	Tongue and groove. Edges form 'V' for better appearing joints. Random lengths.
1.00	UNGLAZED QUARRY TILE	@ .25 / 6"x 6" tile	Useful for countertop or splash rail, or on wall behind wood stove. Heavy to move.
1.09	CEDAR PANELING	@ 34.88/package Covers 32 sq.ft.	Tongue and groove. Edges form 'V' for better appearing joints. Random lengths.
1.23 B	RED BRICK FACING (Real brick, sliced thin)	@ 6.77/carton Covers 5-6 sq.ft.	Use for hearth, or wall behind wood stove. Also to temporarily reface an existing fireplace.
1.76	VICTORIAN SHEET METAL	@ 28.25/panel - Each panel 2 x 8 feet	A revival of the decorative 'tin ceilings' used in turn-of-the-century stores. Has value as Americana.
1.80	HARDWOOD PARQUET (Oak)	⅜" x 12"x 12" @ 1.80 / tile	Pre-stained, two coats urethane varnish and waxed. Can be wall mounted with foam tape.
2.00	CERAMIC TILE (Glazed)	2", 3" or 4" tiles Sold by sq.ft.	Use for counters, and splash rail behind sink. Bathtub caulk makes flexible grout.

PAINT (Nothing else covers a wall for 2 cents a square foot.)

Up against dirty, discolored, or multi-colored walls, your first impulse may be to open the paint can. But hold up a bit. As soon as you get those walls painted one clean color where is your (and everybody's) attention going to be directed? I'll bet it's to those pockmarked window moldings where a dozen different curtain rod holders have held forth. Not to mention those kicked, and scraped-up baseboards. Painting the walls and ignoring the condition of the moldings is like renting formal wear for a party and then forgetting to clean your fingernails.

It follows that some extra effort spent on washing, spackling, and sanding around baseboards, doors, and windows will pay off in a clean look for your finished paint job.

Some day, every good tenant will patch all the holes in the walls when they move. But, the millennium isn't here yet, and the closest I've seen to a miracle is picture hanger holes hurriedly filled with toothpaste!

Spackle plenty. Keep your toothpaste in the medicine cabinet and make a modest investment in one of the truly benign products of Western technology: vinyl spackling paste. Probably no one here remembers when it had to be mixed from scratch, plaster and water, and quickly used before the batch set up. The blessed new stuff comes ready-mixed, stays moist in the can, smells good, is non-toxic, and doesn't shrink — unless you're trying to fill a crater. (You can even fill craters if you build up successive thicknesses, letting each dry until your

fingernail no longer makes an impression.)

A cheap, flexible putty knife and your strong-est index finger are the other tools you'll need. Your finger is what pushes the spackle along cracks where moldings meet walls or floors. (If you're planning to play a flamenco guitar recital in the near future, better save your finger with a tight-fitting rubber glove.) I once spackled every seam in a roomful of board and batten wainscoting, and my spackling finger lost all feeling for two days! Note, in the illustration ② how it's the tip of your finger that gives the neat, rounded shape to the bead of spackle.

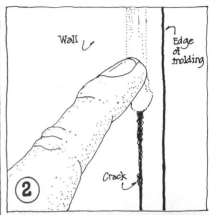

For large, flat areas with nail holes, use the putty knife, and really bear down. The more you feath-er the edges and the less spackle you leave on the wall, the easier will be your sanding chore. If holes are deep, use several thin coats. These will dry faster than a single, thick one ③.

Once, when leaving a rented house and trying to be a responsible tenant, I had already cleaned all the floors before I noticed a plethora of push pin and nail holes in a wall. Not wanting to spackle and sand (because of the dust), and eschewing the old toothpaste trick, I hit upon the idea of spack-ling and then immediately wiping the wall with a damp sponge. Since spackle is water soluble when wet, all but what is trapped in the hole comes smooth-ly away on the sponge. If the spackle is almost dry, dip your sponge in water with a few drops of detergent added. It's quick, and in a white or off-white room, the filled holes are practically invisible. No reason not to use this for moving in, as well as out ④.

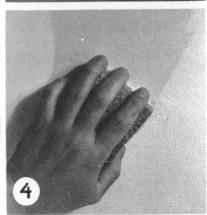

The right paint. Choose latex; period. I could stop with that advice and not lose any sleep over it. Flat latex on walls... semi-gloss latex on woodwork (and walls that must be washed frequently: kitchens; bathrooms)...that combo has done wonders for the places I've lived in. Now I see that *Sears* has an eight year durability warranty on its best interior latex paints. That's not bad, but at *Sears*, or *Montgomery Ward*, or *Penney's*, I'd say buy <u>only</u> the "best." Any paint not guaranteed to cover in one coat should be looked at askance. Not because coverage is so important — in some situations two coats will be needed, never mind what they say — it's simply an indication of the thickness, and therefore the quality of the paint. Price is another indicator: With very few exceptions, a gallon of latex with a list price of less than $8.95 should be avoided. I say list price because, in the West, *Standard Brands* has a flat latex regularly discounted from "$8.95" to $5.95. Except for its strong, and unusually long-lingering odor, it's one of the best paints I've used.

There are still a couple of places where oil-based paints may be worth the trouble. One is on kitchen cabinets, especially the shelves. If you paint the shelves <u>in</u> the cabinets (most of the time they can't be removed) they will dry very slowly because of poor air circulation. If you are eager to put your dishes away and get the hardware back on the drawer-fronts (a perfectly normal and healthy response to chaos) you run the risk of permanently mounting everything. Yup, I know it <u>feels</u> dry, after only an hour or two, but latex paint dries from the outside in. It actually remains fluid (and therefore glue-like) underneath for several weeks!   Oil-based enamel is better for

①

26

surfaces that will have things put on them, because it dries from the inside out. When it's dry to the touch (12 to 18 hours, usually) it's dry enough to use.

The right tools. Up to this point, my recommendations have been mostly according to convention. But now, as I take up the subject of painting tools, I enter a new arena, prepared to do battle with disbelief, outmoded prejudice, and the sting of offended self-interest. <u>Brushes</u>, or <u>Rollers</u>? That is the question. Even the experts don't agree. I painted school interiors one summer under an old-world foreman who had nothing but low, breathy curses for the "amateurs" who painted with rollers. "Too slow!" he said. And I must admit, under his stern gaze we made those six-inch brushes roll right along. (I also recall that everything I ate or drank that summer tasted of semi-gloss enamel.)

For most of my renter's life, though, I have gladly accepted amateur status in exchange for the joy of fumeless,* quick-covering latex-and-roller painting. But being nearsighted, I know that rollers are not my ultimate choice ①.

So, I'm going to dodge the fume-breathing enamel brushers and the many-speckled latex rollers, to step out on a whole new limb. I'm pushing pads.

Pad painting is faster for most people than brushing, and doesn't spatter like rollers. Pad painting is a system. Just as you'd need 2 or 3 different paint brushes to do walls, woodwork, and window mullions, there are different pads for each of these jobs. The basic tool is a flat, 5, 7, or 9-inch wide sponge glued to a plastic platen with a removable handle. The sponge is faced with a synthetic material that looks like a doll-house version of a Flokati rug ②. Pad-painting kits often come with special trays. They're okay, but I wouldn't pay extra for one because there's no trick to what you keep the paint in. If you have an old roller tray, use that. A square, aluminum baking tin works as well. The pad goes flat onto (not into) the surface of the paint. Only dip the "Flokati rug"

* California Air Quality Control Board has recently recommended a ban on the sale of oil-base paints because of the volatility and contribution to air pollution of the mineral spirits used as thinners.

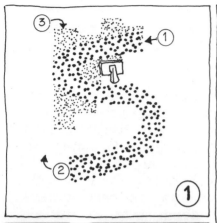

(1)

(2)

SHUR-LINE (3)

avoid getting paint on the sponge. This takes some practice. I had trouble doing <u>anything</u> right at first... dropped one paint-loaded pad on the floor, and was ready to throw the whole works out... but stay with it.

Here's the approach for painting a wall or ceiling with a 7-inch pad: Apply the loaded pad flat to the surface and move it in an "S" pattern. Distribute the paint by stroking across the "S." Then, with a lighter touch, finish off in parallel strokes leading into the previously painted area (1). When you get the dipping and the pressure right, you may be tempted to paint without a dropcloth. That's how clean it <u>feels</u>. But beware. You're about to get cocky, dip a little too much paint, press a bit too hard, and maybe send a big, wet paint blob toward the wall-to-wall carpet.

The large pad has a baby sister – a **mini-pad**. It has some novel uses. The handle slides into a channel at the back of the pad. Let the handle protrude beyond the end of the sponge and it becomes an adjustable guide. Now you can neatly paint window mullions without masking tape (2). Reverse the pad on the handle and you get a tool for painting hard-to-reach areas, like the back edge of a window crossbar (3).

I've saved the best for last: The **paint edger** (4) is a genuine discovery. It is, to painting walls, what a pin-striping tool is to George Barris — a truly liberating device that's suggestive of all kinds of new uses.

What it was made to do is cut straight lines, and this it does, very well.

Now, "cutting" a line with a brush – that is: painting up to a drawn line; a corner; a ceiling; without slopping onto an adjacent area – is an exacting art. It takes lots of practice and a strict avoidance of caffeine. With the edger, you just roll across the wall and it's done, perfectly. There are just a couple of nuances: In place of a "Flokati rug," the paint edger has a kind of low-profile Astro turf. And in the interest of precise control, there is no sponge. You don't dip the edger – you brush paint onto the pad until it has an even, all-over load. This too, needs some patience.

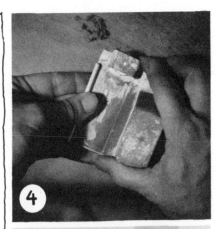

The paint edger is ideal for changing colors at a corner. The position of the pad is adjustable, but for corner painting it should be right up against the stops ④. Start with the edger flat on the wall with the guide wheels contacting the adjacent surface. Regulate pressure (and thereby accuracy) at the "cutting" edge with your index finger. (See how handy digits are?)

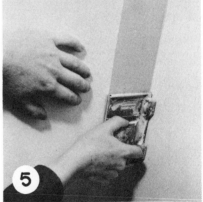

If you've managed to load the pad evenly, you'll discover something neat : As you cut the desired line you also get a bonus : A perfect line at the other side of the edger ⑤. Now you can make contrasting painted moldings around ceilings or floors. You can also make perfect rainbows, or super-size circles with the edger. A hole drilled in the handle, a string and a nail is all it takes ⑥. 🐌

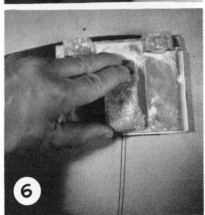

ON AND OFF THE WALL

The next few pages aim to give you a working familiarity with about 20 different wall fasteners. Some are old standards, like push pins and Molly bolts. Others are clever new devices that solve special problems ~ like hanging a picture frame on a brick wall.

You should find here, at least one solution to every kind of hanging task. But it's not an exhaustive list. Any well-stocked hardware store should have all of these and more. Look around and ask. It's worth some effort to get the fastener that lets you do the job neatly, the right way, once.

No Nails. Some rental agreements (both conservative-old, and reactionary-new ones) prohibit nails and nail~like fasteners. College dormitories are usually in this category. So here are some alternatives to the nail:

Push Pins① leave smaller holes than nails and may be tolerated. They are certainly easier on the wall surface than most kinds of tape. Push pins should also be considered when your choices aren't limited. For the greatest holding power, get the long~pointed (⅝") kind and push them up to the hilt, with a twisting motion. You can also tap them in with a small hammer. Properly imbedded, they'll discretely hold posters, lace, even flags recycled from the old lodge hall.

Illustration ② shows push pins used with grommets to hang decorative fabric moldings around the perimeter of a room. More ideas for using push pins, and a complete treatment of "grommetry" can be found under "Curtains for You, Kid," page 136.

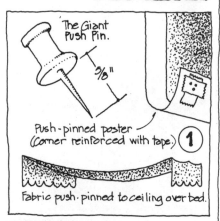

The Giant Push Pin.

⅝"

Push-pinned poster (Corner reinforced with tape.) ①

Fabric push-pinned to ceiling over bed.

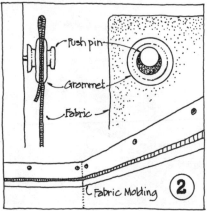

Push pin
Grommet
Fabric
Fabric Molding ②

Staples , like push pins, leave small holes. For big jobs they are cheaper (provided you already own, or can borrow, the stapler) and a little easier to use.

The spring-loaded guns ③ are suitable for plaster-board, wood doors, and wood paneling. Ordinarily you would place the gun flush against the object to be fastened. But keep in mind, you're going to move some day. So experiment—hold the gun so it's floating, about 1/16" above the work. The staple should go almost, but not quite, all the way in, leaving just enough room to wriggle a screwdriver blade under it when it's removal time. Compensate for any loss of holding power by using longer (9/16") staples.

Now, if you are blessed (cursed?) with solid plaster walls, staples shot-from-guns may be too much for them. The impact can spall-off brittle plaster leaving a bombed-out crater instead of the discreet fastening of your dreams.

The solution is to reduce your arsenal. Most ordinary office staplers have a provision for swinging the base away so you can get the business end right against the work ④. This gives you a stapler-tacker that's obedient to the pressure of your hand. You can gently ease staples into crumbly plaster, and in more solid materials you can bang the thing with the heel of your hand and get much the same results as with a gun.

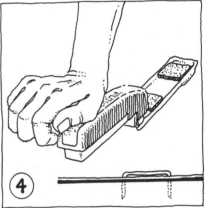

Besides standing-in for push pins, staples are for fastening fabric on wooden stretcher bars, and for covering *Celotex* to make a bulletin board ⑤.

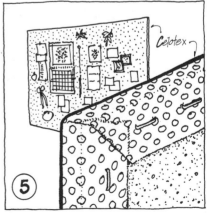

If push pins and staples get you in trouble, there is still hope: **The Interlocking Nail-less Picture Hanger**  is not the little wonder its name suggests, **but** it leaves no holes, and will support mounted posters and picture frames up to 5 pounds. (Some package directions say "up to 15 pounds," but they also warn against hanging anything "breakable or valuable" this way!)

Holding-strength really depends on the wall surface. A smooth, hard surface, like varnished wood paneling, will furnish a much better bond than rough plaster. You can compensate for some unevenness in the surface by supplementing the hanger's water soluble glue with ordinary white glue (such as *Elmer's*).

Removal from the wall is just a matter of holding a wet sponge against

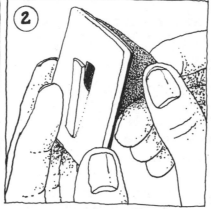

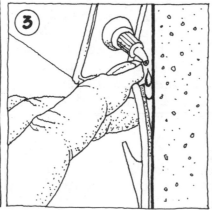

the hanger until the glue softens. Then pull up and off. Wipe away any remaining glue with the sponge.

Stronger (and more expensive) are the new, foam-backed **Self-Adhesive Picture Hooks:** ②. *Magic Mounts* is one brand. They are conservatively rated at five pounds per hanger. Because the tape-like adhesive is so tenacious, the manufacturer doesn't recommend them over wallpaper or plasterboard. The weight of what you're hanging could cause loosely bonded wallpaper to peel and tear.

With plasterboard, the problem comes at removal time. It's possible, in pulling off the hook, to take along a big chunk of the paper covering – right off the gypsum core. Get around this ③ by dripping rubber cement thinner along top edge of the hook, while gently pulling it away from the wall. The solvent will soften the adhesive temporarily, but when it dries the hook is re-usable (with some reduction in holding power). Clean any remaining adhesive from the wall with thinner and a paper towel. Though suggested for plasterboard, this removal technique is a good precaution for any surface.

You can make your own self-adhesive hooks with **Foam Mounting Tape** 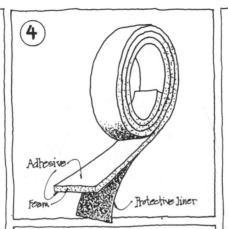. Select hooks with large, flat backs and cut pieces of foam tape to fit. Press firmly into place 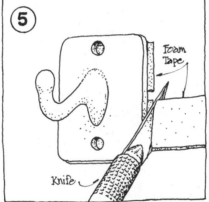. Then remove the protective liner from the tape and stick the hook onto a wall, a refrigerator, a sliding glass door, or almost any clean, smooth surface. It will support a picture frame, light clothing, pot hold-

④

Adhesive

Foam

Protective liner

⑤

Foam Tape

Knife

⑥

Adhesive impregnated balsa

ers and the like, and it's virtually scar-free if you remove it as previously illustrated ③.

Foam tape is also useful for mounting objects directly to the wall. This might include decorative plates, mirror tiles, antique signs, a button collection or almost anything that has a flat back and is reasonably light. (One manufacturer recommends 8 inches of ½-inch wide tape for each pound of weight to be supported. This is very conservative, but it's better to be on the safe side with highly-prized breakables.)

Now, if you want to mount a hook on ceramic tile, foam tape is good, but **Self-Gluing Hooks** ⑥ are stronger. They have a balsa wood backing (to absorb irregularities) and a powerful adhesive activated by water. Dampen the back, press for one minute, and it's set. Let it dry for 24 hours and it's ready to use. The hook can be removed and remounted using glue capsules that you can get from the manufacturer. (See *Selfix* in Shopping Lists.)

In the world of fasteners, the next two items are exotica. Yet there may come a time when you face a unique fastening problem – and the unique solution may just be *Velcro* or magnetic tape.

Velcro is that funny "fish hook" tape that makes great, embarrassing, ripping sounds if you have it on your jacket pockets and try to open them in the movies ①. Here's one possible "home use:" Staple short lengths of *Velcro* "hooks" to a window molding, and sew (or glue) short lengths of *Velcro* "eyes" to a hemmed piece of dark-colored cloth. You've made a neat system that quickly darkens a room for

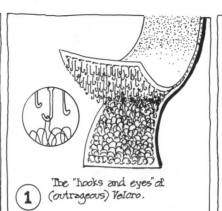

The "hooks and eyes" of (outrageous) Velcro.

①

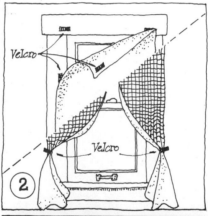

②

③

projecting slides or enlarging negatives ②.

To make a quick-change curtain tie-back, sew or glue one length of *Velcro* to the curtain, and staple a companion length to the window frame ②. *Velcro* is available in fabric stores.

Magnetic Tape is fun to play with, but is it useful? I'm not sure. But for inspiration, I submit my son's invention, a "Magnetic Rabbit, Note-on-the-Refrigerator-Holder" ③. I've also seen this stuff used on a craft bench to hold small knife blades. (End of exotica.)

Picture Moldings are about as hard-to-find as ceilings over eight feet high. But many pre-1920 buildings have them. A friend, raised in suburbia, recently moved into an older urban house. She had lots of framed pictures to hang, but was wary of driving nails into old plaster, so she asked me for ideas. I pointed to the picture moldings in all of the rooms, drew a little diagram of a picture molding hook ④ and she was on her way to the hardware store, amazed and pleased that the problem could be solved without drilling, glueing, or hammering.

There you have it. Nine alternatives to the nail. And not just for those who have sworn to keep their rented walls virginal. Every abode has some surfaces — tile, metal, glass, wood paneling — where nails are not welcome.

Now a couple of "special case" fasteners:

Mirror Holders ⑤ are worth mentioning for two reasons. First, mounting a mirror on the back of a door, or on a medicine cabinet, is a common task. The holders come packaged

④

Picture rail
Picture rail hook
Chain (or nylon fish leader)

Clear plastic mirror holder

⑤

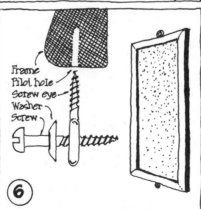

Frame
Pilot hole
Screw eye
Washer
Screw

⑥

with screws suitable for solid wood doors and cabinets. Hollow doors or walls can be handled with the addition of *Togglers*. (See p. 41) Second, plastic mirror holders are still available in an Art Deco style that must have been around for 40 years. How often do you get a chance to buy a bit of Americana off the hardware rack?

Sometimes it's necessary to secure (not just hang) a wooden frame on a wall. Framed bulletin boards and chalkboards are examples. A neat way to do this is to drill a small pilot hole in the top and bottom edges of the frame and then insert screw eyes. A round-headed wood screw goes through each screw eye and into the wall. Check sizes in the store to make sure the screw will nest in the eye and not pull through. Add a finishing washer if there is any doubt ⑥.

Into the wall. There is such a thing as too much respect for the wall surface. The previous pages have preached a gingerliness that is often required of renters. It is also a bit limiting. If you know what you're doing, you can take advantage of some very strong fasteners that go into or through the wall surface, and not risk losing your damage deposit. Property-owners' rules come out of past experiences of dealing with gaping wounds. You're not going to leave gaping wounds, because you're going to know what you're doing. Right?

Knock, Knock. Use your knuckles to give your walls a little physical examination. Hollow walls, like your hollow chest, will give off a dull, empty sound. Solid walls give off a sharp, solid sound, like your head (hopefully).

Most house and apartment

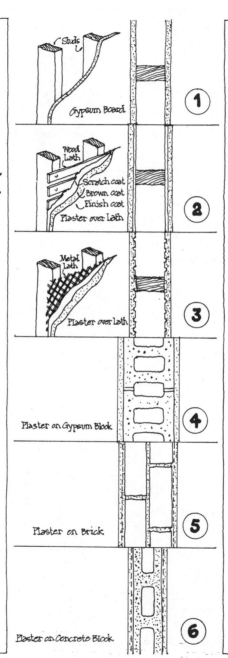

Studs
Gypsum Board ①

Wood Lath
Scratch coat
Brown coat
Finish coat
Plaster over lath ②

Metal Lath
Plaster over lath ③

Plaster on Gypsum Block ④

Plaster on Brick ⑤

Plaster on Concrete Block ⑥

walls are hollow. But that's not all you need to know. Next, you've got to play archeologist. Get a hand or power drill and a small bit (about 1/16 inch). Find an inconspicuous part of the wall, in a corner or behind a couch, and slowly drill a hole. You are going back in time to when your house was built. Watch the dust as it falls from the drill bit. Does it remain white until the drill slides through into empty space? Then you have typical twentieth century gypsum board (also called **plasterboard**, or **sheetrock**. Different names; same item) ①.

But if you get white dust, then tan dust, then wood shavings, you've got turn-of-the-century (and up to about 1920) plaster on wood lath ②, (metal shavings indicate metal lath) ③.

If your wall registered solid in the knocking test, and drilling gives nothing but white dust, you've got either solid plaster, or gypsum blocks (4). A solid wall that yields white, then red dust is plaster over brick or clay tiles (5). White, then gray dust is plaster over concrete (6). Fasteners for all of these solid walls are on pages 43-45.

Hollow wall fasteners.

One of the simplest and least-damaging fasteners for gypsum board and plaster (over lath) walls is an ordinary finishing nail. Driven at an angle, it will hold picture frames up to ten pounds or more. It's easily removable, and the small hole that's left is easy to fill.

The trick is to get the nail exactly where you want it, at the angle you want it. What helps is a firm thumb-and-forefinger grip, and steady tapping from a full-sized hammer. (Light hammers oblige you to swing harder, increasing the chance

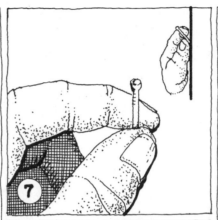

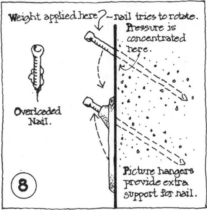

Weight applied here ~ nail tries to rotate.
Pressure is concentrated here.

Overloaded Nail.

(8)

Picture hangers provide extra support for nail.

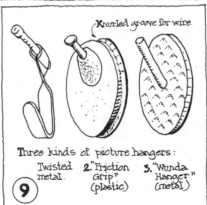

Knurled groove for wire.

Three kinds of picture hangers:
(9) 1. Twisted metal. 2. "Friction Grip" (plastic) 3. "Wunda Hanger" (metal)

of missing or bending the nail (7).

But there's one thing that can bring the downfall (quite literally) of the finishing nail: Too much weight. In a contest of wills between the side of a nail (bearing surface) and the plaster or gypsum wall, the wall loses (8).

Enter the **picture hanger**, a generic name for a whole crop of improvements on the finishing nail. There are many designs, but all have a common purpose: To distribute the weight from the nail to a bigger chunk of the wall (9). As a bonus, they also help hold the nail at the proper angle while you pound it in.

Any of these hangers can be removed just as you would pull an ordinary nail. Pry up on the nail head with the claws of the hammer, using a thin scrap of wood to protect the wall.

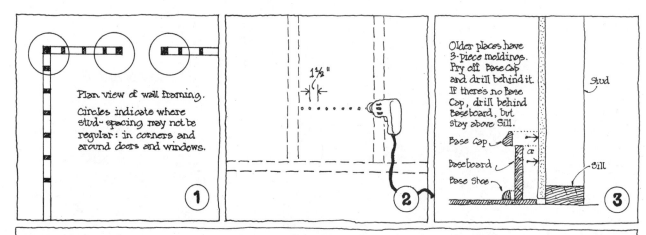

Plan view of wall framing.

Circles indicate where stud-spacing may not be regular: in corners and around doors and windows. ①

1½" ②

Older places have 3-piece moldings. Pry off Base Cap and drill behind it. If there's no Base Cap, drill behind Baseboard, but stay above Sill.

Base Cap
Baseboard
Base Shoe

Stud
Sill ③

Locating studs.

Inside every gypsum board or lath and plaster wall are some sturdy wooden columns called studs. They're strong enough to support a basketball backboard; but if that's not in your plans, think what ideal supports they could be for shelves full of heavy books and records. The only problem is the studs are behind the wall. And the part of the wall with a stud behind it looks just like the part without a stud behind it.

Now I've tried lots of different techniques for locating studs. I've tried sounding them out by tapping all along the wall with my knuckles. I've used magnetic stud finders. I've even examined the wall with a flashlight, trying to detect slight bulges where it passes over the studs. And still I've ended up drilling lots of near-miss holes in the wall.

So my seasoned advice is to avoid all the hunting and doubting, and go for the drill right away. Find an inconspicuous spot near the middle of the wall.* You're trying to determine the pattern for all the studs ~ so you stay away from corners of the room where the pattern may vary ①.

Drill in a horizontal line, moving over 1½ inches for each new hole ②. Assuming you're unlucky enough to have drilled the first hole just past a stud, you will need to drill no more than 10 holes before you hit paydirt. (Standard stud spacing is 16 inches center-to-center. Some older buildings will have 12-inch stud spacing, and some cottages, barns, etc., have studs 24 inches "on center.")

---

*You may be able to completely hide your exploratory drilling by prying off baseboard moldings ③. In any case, the small holes are easy to patch.

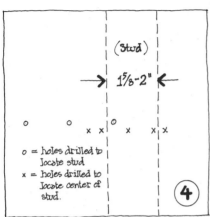

(Stud)

←→ 1⅝-2"

o   o   x x|o x   x|x

o = holes drilled to
   locate stud
x = holes drilled to
   locate center of
   stud.

④

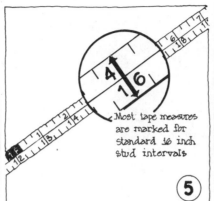

Most tape measures
are marked for
standard 16 inch
stud intervals

⑤

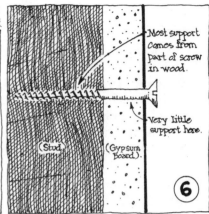

Most support
comes from
part of screw
in wood.

(Stud)   (Gypsum
          board).

Very little
support here.

⑥

Once you find a stud, poke around a bit with your drill to get its exact position. (Studs are 1½ to 2 inches wide.) When you've found the outside edges, you can determine the center, and from there you can measure (16 inches) to the center of the next stud. Drill there too, as a check on whether you have standard spacing ④. (If not – sorry – you've got to drill another series of holes starting from the stud you found. Keep going until you find that non-conforming second one.) Now you can locate all the other studs in the wall just by measuring ⑤.

Peptalk. If you're reading this and stud-hunting for the first time, you may be feeling overwhelmed by it all. Don't despair. You are developing a new sense; one that will enable you to see through your walls and tap their hidden strength. Such power doesn't come easily. But it's well worth having.

Wall power. Previously, you might have thought of the floor as the support for your furniture, and the walls as simply the boundaries of the floor. With the studs as an ally, you can begin to think of the wall as an _extension_

of the floor; another support for furnishings, and a way to open up your room-arranging options. There's more on this idea throughout the book, and especially in "Shaker Walls" p.150.

Fasteners for studs.
Studs are wood. And therefore most common wood fasteners – nails, wood screws, lag screws – can be put into studs. There are just a couple of things to remember:
1: The first part of the fastener reaches through ½ to ⅝ inch of crumbly plaster or soft gypsum board ⑥. Not much support

there. So choose a length that will go through the gypsum or plaster, and at least 1½ inches into the stud. And 2, studs are hard. You'll have a tough time driving even a small wood screw without drilling a **pilot hole**. Pilot holes provide space for the core of the screw, letting the threads do a better job of gripping ①. I usually use the "eyeball" method to determine the correct drill size for pilot holes. Looked at from the side (closing one eye may help) the drill bit diameter should be slightly less than the diameter of the core of the screw ①.

Lag screws * ② are sort of overgrown wood screws. Instead of screwdriver slots, they have hexagonal heads so they can be turned with a wrench. A lag screw driven into a pilot hole is one of the strongest connections you can make to a wall stud. Add a washer, and it's a good-looking connector, too.

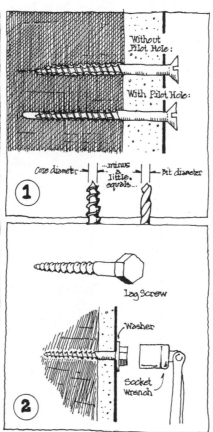

Without Pilot Hole:

With Pilot Hole:

Core diameter — ...minus little. equals... — Bit diameter

①

Lag Screw

Washer

Socket Wrench

②

Ledger running between three studs supporting a row of hooks:

Bookcase supported by ledger.

③

A **ledger** ③ is not a specific thing so much as an <u>idea</u>, with wide applications. It's any board working like a bridge and also like a shelf. As a bridge, it can span between two, three, or more studs, transferring a load placed anywhere along its length (the shelf analogy) to the strong connectors at the studs.

Nails are of limited usefulness in attaching to studs because they are difficult to remove without damaging the wall surface. The exception to this is attaching wood moldings. Finishing nails driven into studs are the choice here, because they virtually disappear when filled with wood putty ④. Prying off the molding will usually bring the nails out too. If they insist on pulling through the wood and staying in the wall, use a claw hammer and pry against a scrap-wood block ④. See also "Coming to the Edge," p. 54.

* Also called lag <u>bolts</u>.

No studs. Because the world is sometimes an imperfect place, you won't always have a stud where you want to hang something heavy. For these trying times there are...

Hollow wall anchors. They come in different styles: plastic, metal expansion-type (Molly's) and toggle bolts. I greet any modernization of standard hardware items with suspicion; especially plastic standing in for metal. But I've been using a plastic wall anchor called *The Toggler* and I like it a lot. It does a few things better than a Molly (see p. 42) and it's easier to install.

Togglers ⑤ come in hooks and flush-mount models. Mounting is similar for both. First, drill the hole-size recommended on the package. Then fold the prongs of the *Toggler* together and push it into the hole. Tap the fastener flush to the wall with a scrap of dowel and a

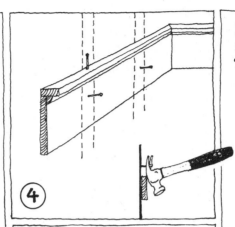

④

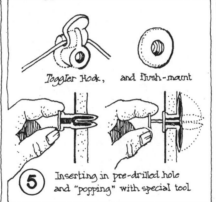

Toggler Hook, and *flush-mount*

⑤ Inserting in pre-drilled hole and "popping" with special tool

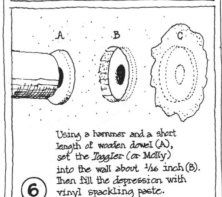

⑥ Using a hammer and a short length of wooden dowel (A), set the *Toggler* (or Molly) into the wall about 1/16 inch (B). Then fill the depression with vinyl spackling paste.

hammer. Using the special plastic tool that's provided, "pop" the prongs into the open, locked-behind-the-wall position. Insert the screws supplied, or use longer, wood or sheet metal screws. The choice depends on the thickness of what you're mounting. If fatter screws are needed, the hole in the *Toggler* can be enlarged somewhat by drilling.

Here are two good things about *Togglers*: First; when tapped flush, the milky plastic flange takes on the color of the wall and almost disappears. Second; built-in fins behind the flange keep the Toggler from turning when you drive in the screw. (If you're using the *Toggler* hook, be sure it's straight up before these fins engage the wall.)

Neither *Togglers* or Molly's are as removable as you are. The best way to make them go is to simply pound them on into the wall ⑥.

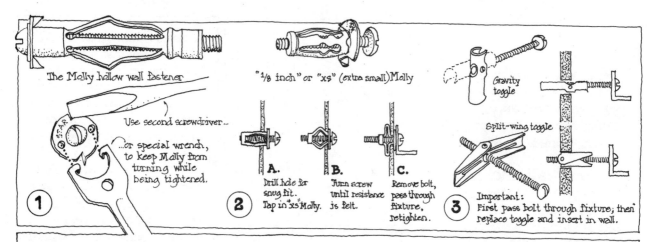

The Molly hollow wall fastener

Use second screwdriver...

...or special wrench, to keep Molly from turning while being tightened.

(1)

"⅛ inch" or "xs" (extra small) Molly

A. Drill hole for snug fit. Tap in "xs" Molly.

B. Turn screw until resistance is felt.

C. Remove bolt, pass through fixture, retighten.

(2)

Gravity toggle

Split-wing toggle

Important: First pass bolt through fixture; then replace toggle and insert in wall.

(3)

Molly was once the trade-name for a patented wall fastener (as *Toggler* is today). When the patent expired, several manufacturers came out with similar designs but called them by different names. No one was taken in by this. In the parlance of tradespeople, any wall anchor that looks like a Molly is still called a Molly.

Mollys are really more like bolts than screws (though "Molly screw" is also heard). To use one, you first drill a hole that will be a snug fit for the collar (2)**A.** Then insert the Mol-

ly (screw-and-all) and tap it flush to the wall. Next, turn the screw. This draws the threaded part of the flange toward the screw head and opens an "umbrella" of steel fingers against the back of the hollow wall. In real life, you won't be able to see all this ingenious stuff happening, but illustration 2 should at least feed your imagination.

Meanwhile, you had better keep your eyes on the flange, to make sure it's not turning along with the screw. To prevent this, you'll need a second screwdriver, or the

special little wrench that's included with some packaged Mollys (1). When all is tight, the screw must be backed out, put through whatever's to be hung, and then reinstalled.

For aesthetic reasons, and because Mollys are a little more difficult to install, I prefer *Togglers* for most situations. But if I'm dealing with hollow-core doors, or thin wood paneling, I like the extra-small Molly (2). *Toggler* makes a special hollow door fastener too, but in my experience, the Molly makes a more positive connection to these thin materials.

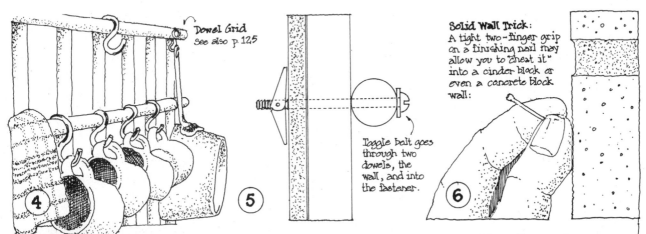

Dowel Grid
See also p. 125

Toggle bolt goes
through two
dowels, the
wall, and into
the fastener.

Solid Wall Trick:
A tight two-finger grip
on a finishing nail may
allow you to "cheat it"
into a cinder block or
even a concrete block
wall:

④

⑤

⑥

Toggle bolts ③ are the Mack Trucks of hollow wall fasteners. They cost a bit more; they're stronger; and they come in bigger sizes than *Togglers* or *Mollys*. Toggle bolts are the best choice when you have thick and/or especially heavy things to hang on a wall and there's no stud in the vicinity.

For example, suppose you're mounting the dowel grid shown in ④. Even though the grid is based on 16-inch stud-spacing it's possible the (best laid) plans will run amok and you won't be able to go into studs.

What are the options? The screws that come with Mollys and *Togglers* are not long enough to go through the dowel and into the fastener, too. You could substitute longer screws; you could recess the head of the shorter screw; or (get ready) *you could choose a toggle bolt that's the correct length to begin with!* ⑤.

It works that way with toggle bolts. For some jobs they're the perfect choice. But most of the time they'll take a back seat to *Togglers* and *Mollys*.

Solid walls. Thin plaster over brick; exposed brick; concrete; cinder block — how do you attach to these? Not too long ago your only choices were to buy or borrow a masonry bit, a heavy-duty power drill, and start boring holes in the wall. Or you could try your luck with masonry nails — a not always successful, and often-times downright destructive alternative.

For hanging really heavy objects that's still all we've got. But now, thanks again to modern plastics, there is an ingeniously simple way to attach lightweight things (up to 25 pounds per fastener) to solid walls. The patented devices are imported by the *Moore Push Pin Company,* and they have a variety of configurations and names, all beginning with "hard surface wall..."

The Hard surface wall Picture Hanger is representative of the series

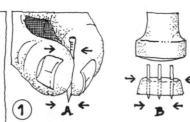

(2). Like the others, it has a thick plastic body containing an array of supersharp hardened steel pins — in this instance, four of them.

The way these hangers work is a bit like the old trick for getting a thin nail into hard wood: You'd squeeze the shaft of the nail really hard between thumb and forefinger, and rap the nail head smartly. Most of the time the nail would not bend because of the "collar" of support your fingers provided (1). (The nailing trick (6) on the previous page is the same idea.)

Hard Surface Wall... Picture Hanger.
Hang picture frames, plaques, kitchen utensils, small tools.

"Thumbtack."
Use like push-pins for hanging illustrations, posters, tapestries, flags. Also use as wall protection bumpers.

Utility Clip.
Hang small pictures, light mirrors, wiring, decorations.

Hanger Loop.
Hang wire, lightweight pipe, climbing plants.

Staple.
Hang wiring, Christmas decorations, lightweight signs, wire cloth.

Fastening Plate.
Attach lighting fixtures, wall clocks, lightweight cabinets and shelves.

In a similar way the thick plastic of the hard surface wall fastener provides a collar of support that directs all the force of the hammer blows straight to each steel point (1B). This, plus the sharpness of the points, allows penetration of hard surfaces without the nails bending or the material cracking.

The picture hanger is only one of six different hard surface wall fasteners currently available. The five others and their uses are shown in (3).

Any of these fasteners can be removed by slipping a thin knife blade (an old kitchen knife is ideal) between wall and fastener and prying off gently. If the nail points are not obviously blunted you may be able to reuse the fastener.

Notes and cautions.
Hard surface wall fasteners will only support weight that pulls straight

down. They're not in-
tended for solid plaster
walls, thick plaster (more
than 1/8 inch) over masonry, or plaster over lath.
Nor are they suitable
for tile, Formica, very
hard brick, or very hard
natural stone.

The end is near. That's 15
pages of fasteners and a
mere scratch on the sur-
face of a deep subject.
But having scratched at
all, I don't want to
leave any wall mounting
problems still itching.

So what do you do with...
**Solid plaster, hard con-
crete, brick, and stone?**
Solid plaster is too soft
and crumbly to nail or
screw into; some brick,
stone, and concrete is too
hard (even for hard sur-
face fasteners). The solution for both situations is
to drill a hole in the wall.
Then insert a **wall plug,**
which will obligingly en-
large and wedge itself
into the hole as its
screw or bolt is tight-
ened (4). In the case of

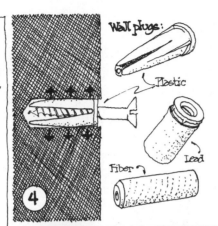

Wall plugs:

Plastic

Lead

Fiber?

(4)

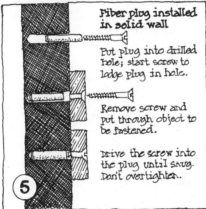

Fiber plug installed
in solid wall

Put plug into drilled
hole; start screw to
lodge plug in hole.

Remove screw and
put through object to
be fastened.

Drive the screw into
the plug until snug.
Don't overtighten.

(5)

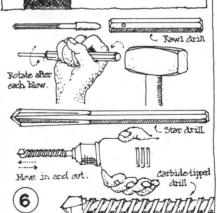

Rawl drill

Rotate after
each blow.

star drill

Move in and out.

Carbide-tipped
drill

(6)

solid plaster, the plug
can be fiber or plastic
and the drilling can be
done with the same
drill and bit you'd use
for wood (5).

Concrete, stone, and brick
call for more specialized
equipment. It's the kind
of stuff you'll want to
rent or borrow. For holes
smaller than 1/4 inch
you can drill (slowly) by
hand with a **rawl drill.**
A **star drill** is a hand
operated drill for holes
up to 1 inch. Rotate the
rawl or star drill about
a quarter turn after each
blow of the hammer.
Hold the drill with a
gloved hand and definite-
ly wear goggles. For more
speed use a **carbide-
tipped drill** bit along
with an industrial-type
1/2 inch power drill (6).

Plugs for holes in masonry
can be fiber, plastic, or
lead. Lead anchors have
the advantage of being
threaded for bolts, and
that includes heavy-duty
screw eyes and hooks. ▪

45

WALL DRESSING

One box in my moving kit carries an especially valuable payload. It's labeled "Hangings," and it contains folded cotton prints, my bedspread from when I was a kid, two quilts, and a small Navajo rug. This is the first box I unpack if I want to quickly put the stamp of my own personality on a new place. These materials are lightweight, they have sound-dampening and insulating qualities, as well as a comfortable aesthetic.

The subtly-colored Navajo rug ① is one of my special treasures. (It was a Christmas present—a unique gift that looks like it will travel with me for years.) This classic rug looks good on wood floors, or on top of wall-to-wall carpets. But as its value balloons upward (along with the cost of cleaning) it has achieved the inflated status of "wall hanging." In the same way, my appreciation for old quilts has increased to the point where putting one on a bed, at the risk of wear and fading, is out of the question. In my present bedroom, the bed wears a plain blue dacron-filled comforter. ② The soon-to-be antique quilt is safely on the wall.

But you don't have to collect old things to enjoy the warmth and adaptability of fabrics on the walls. *Marimekko* is a Finnish maker of bold and richly colored cotton prints that are perfect for wall hangings. They cost between ten and fifteen dollars per yard, but for this rather steep initial investment you get a lasting and versatile hanging. The pure, intense colors and simple designs don't become boring, so *Marimekko* travels well from abode to abode. And the colors are so sen-

sitively combined that you can use the fabric as a start toward choosing colors for a whole room. I painted one wall of an otherwise all-white room to match the deep green in a *Marimekko* print. A dresser mirror placed against the green wall reflects the print on the opposite wall, so wall and print are sometimes seen together, sometimes apart. This simple correspondence gives an ordinary room a chance at some distinction.

You can make your own quilt-like wall-hangings by sewing together things that are usually separate. Look for pot holders at the thrift shops and flea markets. Buy several at a time to get a better price. You can always cover the worn or strange-colored ones with new material. Combine the old potholders with new, dimestore versions in solid colors or bright prints. Holders of different sizes and shapes can be "floated" on a ground of solid color. (Blue denim is complimentary to the colors in most pot holders ③.)

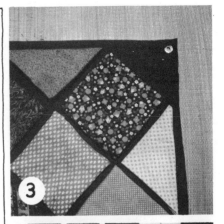

For many moves, I carried along a sort of quilt-without-padding made from maritime signal flags. I bought a string of them, each about 12 x 15 inches, at a ship chandlery. I removed the string and sewed the flags edge-to-edge in a pleasing graphic arrangement. A folded muslin basting sewn to the top edge, plus brass grommets, for hanging, completed the project ④. (In my last rented house the flag collage served as a drape over an otherwise open closet.)

My friend, Bonnie, collects embroidered patches, and has grouped some of them for display in a picture frame ⑤. They'd also look good tack-sewn

FABRIC GLUE

Don't shy away from using fabrics simply because you don't sew. There are several good fabric glues and iron-on tapes on the market. Best source is the notions section of a large variety store. Look for *Elmer's Fabric Mender* cement, *Barge All Purpose* cement, or *Tal-A-Tear Greeze* fabric cement. *Bondex Fusing Strip* is one brand of iron-on mending tape.

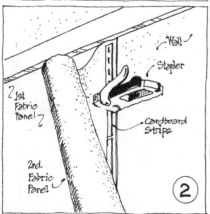

or glued to a large panel of fabric. Blue denim is a good choice here, too. A great array of patches is available.— rainbows, railroad emblems, car marques, stars and stripes, etc. Try sewing notions departments, hobby shops, and surplus stores. Also check the Yellow Pages for "fraternal regalia."

Wallcloth. Fabric can also be used to cover an entire wall. Using muslin or denim or sale-priced cotton prints brings the cost about even with wallpaper. And, unlike wallpaper, cloth covers just about anything and uncovers it again when you move.

Heavy, non-stretch fabrics like denim, artist's canvas and even burlap can be applied directly to smooth walls. Just measure the wall to be covered (width and height) and multiply to get the total square footage. Buy about five percent extra for seams, and ten to twenty percent extra if a large repeating pattern must be matched.

Use a plumb bob (or simply a scissors tied to a long string) as a guide for getting the first panel straight (1). Cut each panel to the height of the wall plus an inch extra at the top and bottom.

Turn under that inch at the top of the first panel and hang it parallel to the plumb line. Use a staple gun and 5/16 inch staples (see p. 31) to fasten it at the top and along the sides. Fold the extra fabric under at the bottom and staple that last. (2)

Start the second panel backside out and in all-

48

over contact with the first panel ③. Staple it in several places along the edge where the two panels meet. Along that same edge, staple ½ inch wide strips cut from shirtboards (from the laundry) or poster board (art supply store). Check these strips again with the plumb line. as they are fastened.

Now pull the second panel over the line of cardboard strips and you will have made a neat, hidden seam ④. Staple the other edge of the second panel and proceed in the same manner along the wall.

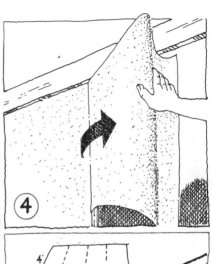

④

Fabric "tiles." A more easily reclaimable fabric wall is made by wrapping cloth around modular sections cut from ½ inch insulation board ⑤. Cover the "tiles" with enough fabric to wrap the edges and extend onto the back an inch or two. Fasten the panels with one or two finishing nails. Because the panels are so light it's usually not necessary to drive the nails into studs. At moving time, pry off the panels. The nails will pull through and stay in the wall for easy extraction. A quilt-like variation on this same idea involves cutting the insulation board into hexagons and wrapping them with a homey selection. of plain or patterned cottons. You can cover an entire wall, or just do a small section ⑥.

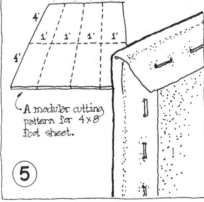

A modular cutting pattern for 4 × 8 foot sheet.

⑤

An encouraging word. Wall hangings are where you find them. It sometimes just takes imagination to see the familiar in a new role. Be on the lookout for: fraternal flags, banners, lace tablecloths, Peruvian shawls, East Indian wedding banners, and so on ... 🐦

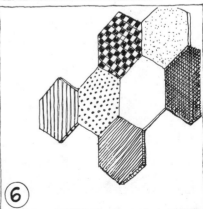

⑥

Frame Ups

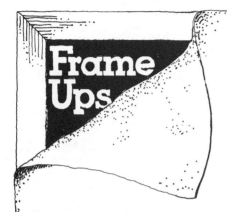

1

2

Frames may seem like a rather self-evident component of the portable life. If there's innovation here, it's in a way of <u>thinking</u> about frames.

I've already mentioned my friend Bonnie's embroidered patch collection ①. The point to be made here is that it's the frame that makes a collection like this happen. Stashed away in a drawer, or in an unopened packing box, it tells us nothing about its owner/assembler, nor does it give <u>her</u> much pleasure. In the frame it's still protected, doesn't collect much dust, and always draws <u>my</u> attention. Each one of these patches has a little story behind it, and I now know some of them.

Not everyone collects embroidered patches. But many of us rootless wanderers are carrying around family snapshots and family albums. I was, but I moved them several times, and never unpacked them. I think it took seeing Jacques Lartigue's snapshots—in the impressive collection published by the Museum of Modern Art—to jog my awareness of the beauty and value of my own collection. This is a valuable visual resource for any individual or family, but especially for those who move frequently.

A wall of family memorabilia can be a centering influence for children who move. And asking them to help assemble and frame the collection, including some of their artwork, makes it a shared experience of continuity; a warm tonic for the feelings of disorientation that often accompany a move.

The framing of art by children is an art in itself. Since kids usually paint or draw right to the edge of the paper, cutting a window in a mat board means blocking some of their creation from view. What seems to work better is to choose a frame considerably larger than the art. Cut a mat to fit the frame and mount the drawing on the face of the mat using double-stick tape along the top back edge only. Secure the mat tightly against the glass. The art will be flat but still able to expand and contract without wrinkling. And the original will be in full view, edges and all, just as the artist conceived it ③.

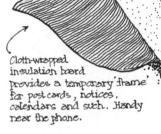

Cloth-wrapped insulation board provides a temporary 'frame' for post cards, notices, calendars and such. Handy near the phone.

Old photos look good in old frames. It's also cheaper that way. Find old frames at thrift shops, garage sales and the like. If the frame itself is in good shape, it's most likely a bargain compared to a new one. Old, intact glass can be brightened up with a razor blade scraper and window cleaner. Mats and backing can be replaced.

Some memorabilia is too transient for framing. Post cards, snapshots, notices, and clippings are collectibles with shorter lives. I give this material a semblance of order by preparing one big, pinboard home for it. A piece of insulation board wrapped with a tiny flower or geometric cotton print is all it takes ④.

When I move, the framed treasures are among the first items to be packed. They go on edge in boxes (orange crates for the larger ones) with folded newspapers or folded towels and sheets separating them. These boxes travel on the back seat of a car rather than in a moving truck. These suggestions are only a beginning. The operating principle is to look for items with personal history and significance, frame them for visibility and protection, and enjoy them. ❧

LITTLE WORLDS

I've noticed that people who move a lot (and stay sane) often permit themselves one or two mild insanities. My friend Jay, for example, has moved 8 times in the past 10 years, but wouldn't think of selling his piano. I guess I've got a bad case too. I deny my nomadic existence by collecting old light bulbs and laboratory glass. This stuff couldn't be more fragile, but I pack it every time with loving care, and take great pride in having moved it five times now without a crack.

Even if you're not a light bulb collector, the display box I built for my glassware may start an idea for you. It's made from 3/8 × 4 inch redwood bender board, but 1/4 to 1/2 inch pine, or even lumber salvaged from a fruit crate, would do as well. There's

Screw eyes for hanging

Fabric-covered back, cut to fit inside opening.

Dimensions depend on items to be displayed.

1¼" brad.

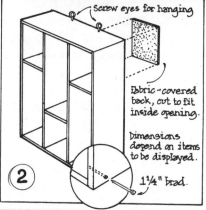

nothing fancy about the construction. Simple butt joints are fastened with white glue and finishing nails. (Nails are driven into smaller pre-drilled holes to avoid splitting the thin wood.) A back for the shelves is optional. I cut individual backs for each opening and wrapped them in different-colored fabrics ①.

Cartoonist Phil Frank put together this collage in a recycled "California job case" ③. These well-crafted hardwood drawers once held complete alphabets of metal type, but they've been made obsolete by computer-set phototypography. You'll see them turning up in antique stores with up-to-date prices, but a little snooping around a small-town newspaper office/job printer may net you some, free.

Phil's idea was to mount the type case on the wall before he had enough items for all the niches. After that, it sort of completed itself.

His kids collected stones and seashells. Friends brought small contributions as house gifts. And for the rest, Phil claims that in his flea market wanderings, nifty little collectibles would occasionally jump out at him and beg to be included.

Type cases are not the only drawers that can be given a second chance. Consider salvaging wooden drawers from old built-in kitchen cabinets. (The kind that held silverware will already be subdivided.) Look for these in second-hand stores and in salvage yards that deal in used building materials. (4)

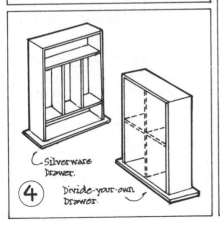

Silverware Drawer.

④ Divide-your-own Drawer.

⑤ The Classic 12 bottle Soda Crate.

The wooden soda-bottle crate is another functional item that has suddenly become collectible. The switch to metal and plastic crates is complete, but the wooden ones are still around and (as yet) too plentiful to bring fancy prices. Hung on a wall with their original graphics intact, these boxes make a good home for nature treasures, sewing supplies, old toys, etc.

Designer Bill Wells orchestrated the assemblage of *Seven-Up* and *Pepsi* crates shown in 6. This is only one of three similar walls that surround his drawing table. He uses the 4-inch-square pigeon holes in the

Pepsi crates for ink bottles, pens and other art supplies. (The spaces between boxes don't go to waste either.) The *Seven-Up* boxes are deeper, and didn't come with dividers. Bill uses some of these "as is," and in others he's put in his own dividers. 1 x 12 inch boards provide some extra structure. Three years ago, Bill got all the crates (25 cents each) from a Los Angeles supermarket.

The final word: indulge. Collecting seems to be a natural part of nestbuilding. And creating little worlds in boxes is not a bad antidote to the big, chaotic world outside.

⑥

COMING TO THE EDGE

What has become of all the "Little Boxes" — those endless rows of pink, yellow and blue tract houses that Malvina Reynolds derided in her famous 60's folk song? Well, some of them have grown up to become rental units. Don't laugh. There aren't enough "charming older homes" for all of us. And even if there were, there's still something to be said for the adequate wiring, sufficient plumbing, and workable kitchens you usually find in these post-war tract houses.

What you don't find is character, and individuality. But it's possible to put back some of those qualities that modern expedience-architecture has stripped away. And you can do it with less effort (and more satisfaction) than it would take to deal with an old-house bugaboo like faulty plumbing.

Missing Moldings. It's not just the low ceilings that make modern rooms oppressive. It's the lack of definition between walls and ceilings and floors. In short, no moldings (or only narrow, nearly invisible ones). Real moldings— at the floor, at the ceiling, and sometimes around the middle of rooms — are like furniture. They impart a human scale. But real moldings are also expensive, and not very portable.

Trompe L'oeil. That's the French term for paintings so realistic they "fool the eye." It also suggests a way to get the visual effect of moldings without the cost. You simply paint them in. A four inch wide stripe at the top of the wall is about right. Six to eight inches is a good dimension for a base (floor-level) molding. Color choice is important. Warmth can be added to a stark white room by painting in moldings in a yellow ochre or reddish-brown wood-like color. The painted molding might also echo the color in a brick fireplace or in a prominent piece of furniture. Painting a wide base molding the same color as the floor (or floor covering) will make the room look visually larger. I find the easiest, fastest way to paint neat moldings is with a "paint edger" (see p.28).

Moveable Moldings. Paint is cheap, but laborious if you have to first paint the moldings in, then paint them out when you move. Fabric strips involve more initial work, but they are reclaimable. If you make them in unit lengths, like four or six feet, they'll adapt to just about any room you come across. Hemming can be done with a machine, with fabric cement, or with strips of iron-on tape ④. Make extra strips, or at least save some of the unhemmed material, in case the next assignment is in a larger room. I think you'll find solid colors are best for this use. The printed pattern you choose for this room may not work in the next one, and you're likely to tire of a print more quickly.

Illustration ⑤ shows a "real" molding I put up in my present, rented house. The wood was finished to complement the table and it helps warm up an otherwise sterile dining corner. As you can see it also serves as a display rail and a chair rail. (Backs of chairs rub this instead of scoring the wall.) It's all held in place with a minimum number of finishing nails driven into studs. You can be sure I won't be leaving this behind when I move. It may have to be cut. but I'm sure I'll find a use for it in my next place. ✎

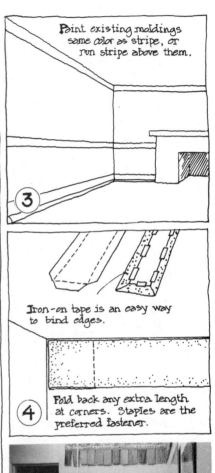

Paint existing moldings same color as stripe, or run stripe above them.

③

Iron-on tape is an easy way to bind edges.

Fold back any extra length at corners. Staples are the preferred fastener.

④

⑤

Install a Wall

Renters and rentals — it's tough to get a perfect fit between the two. Homebuyers must also do some compromising, but they enjoy the option of changing things, even knocking out a wall if need be. There's really no reason renters can't also do some manipulation of space. Removing walls is out. But who's to say they can't <u>add</u> some?

Here are five suggestions for dividing and conquering space problems, with walls you install yourself.

Doors become walls. Hollow-core doors are lightweight, stable, and inexpensive. <u>Quite</u> inexpensive if you find your way to your lumberyard's damaged door department. Here, for five to ten dollars, you can pick up doors with loose veneer (it can be glued back on), or with holes in the veneer (they can be covered over). Doors become partitions, strictly speaking, rather than walls, because they're only 6 feet - 8 inches tall. But this is fine where you want just visual privacy, as in a bedroom shared by two kids. The plan ① shows four doors bracketed together into a free-standing unit that separates the beds. Doors are fastened, top and bottom, with metal mending plates and wood screws ②. Canvas, burlap, or cotton fabric can be stretched over the doors, and stapled along the edges. This is better done before fastening the panels together. If the veneers are in good shape, staining or painting the doors is another possibility.

Wall that is not a wall. It took me only a few minutes to push-pin a lace tablecloth to the ceiling and tack it to the back of the bed, but the change in my

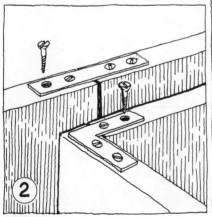

1. Diagonal placement of beds and partition adds interest; Works for 10 x 12 ft. and larger rooms.

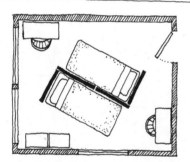

2.

bedroom is remarkable ③. Instead of a room at the end of a short hallway, there are two rooms: A now-useful dressing area in front of the closet, and a bedroom with greater privacy. In the daytime, with the drapes open, the lace passes natural light to the closet, but still screens the view from outside.

Furniture walls. In ④A a worktable is isolated from the rest of the bedroom by backing it against a dresser. Hanging fabric hides the unfinished back of the dresser and reinforces the visual division of space. In ④B bookshelves mark off a dining area. The back of the shelves is made interesting with a hanging rug. A cotton print or a group of framed pictures would work as well.

Window walls. It's the largest open space in my rented house; a two-car basement-garage that contains: **1.** A woodworking shop; **2.** A graphic design studio; and **3.** An animation stand. That means sawdust, india ink, and movie film, all in the same area—not a good mixture. The problem was to isolate the workshop, and not lose the openness. I needed a wall that would transmit light, but not dust. This seemed impossibly ambitious for a renter, until I came upon the solution in a debris box: Two garage doors (victims of a remodeling project) each with nine windows — all the glass intact.

The photograph ⑤ shows the doors in place. They're framed with 2x4 inch lumber and sealed at the top with a strip of heavy-duty polyethylene. Everything is nailed or stapled in place in a minimal way. It's removable, it looks good, and it works. ✍

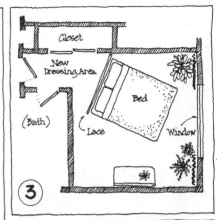

③

④

⑤

2
Lighting Up

A four-year-old I know loves to come into a room full of adults and hit the light switch—plunging the whole place into darkness. The reactions range from bemused tolerance—"Kids will be kids"—to grumbling indignation—"Why doesn't somebody discipline that child!" But nobody, including the four-year-old, misses the real point: For a moment, this small child has stolen all the thunder from a gathering of the elders, and she's done it with just a flick of a finger. Like it or not, everyone in the room gets a fresh awareness of what powerful instruments technology gives us, and of how reluctant we are to toy with them.

Lighting really is powerful. But it needn't always be remote and inhuman. Our public spaces all seem to have lighting designed to military specifications. The imperative is "Eliminate All Shadows!" Like Muzak, light is forced into every crack and crevice.

Home lighting is not much better. Because electricity and light bulbs were scarce at first, early twentieth-century homes got only one fixture per room. Sensibly (democratically), it was placed where it would do the widest possible good—dead center in the ceiling. Regrettably, this practice is still with us. Even in contemporary houses and apartments, only the "living room" is spared the central fixture.

Luckily, lighting is easy, even fun to change. The tools you'll need are minimal, and the materials are well-designed and neatly interchangeable. (In this, the U.S. has it all over Europe and England, where plugs and sockets come in a bewildering, nonstandardized array.) To me, the electrical section of the hardware store is like one giant bin of Erector Set parts. Unlike plumbing supplies and car parts, everything fits (or can be easily adapted) to everything else.

Wiring is also relatively goof-proof. Anyone, with the aid of a friend, can master the breaker panel (or fuse box) where electricity is shut off for each circuit being worked on. (See p. 62.) The other shibboleth is to take careful note (a drawing may help) of which wires go to the fixture you're replacing. You'll want to connect the new fixture to exactly the same wires.

But a little fear is healthy. To paraphrase the old saw about mushroom hunters: "There are no old, bold electricians." If your house is very different from the examples shown here, or if you get more ambitious, get yourself grounded (not literally) with a good book on basic home wiring. 🐌

The Right Light

After recklessly advocating the overthrow of the central ceiling fixture, I thought I'd better come up with some positive alternatives. So, on this page, a three-part "manifesto" on <u>thinking</u> about lighting. And following that, more about <u>doing</u>.

Task Lighting ①. Some activities — sewing and studying are examples — demand high levels of concentrated brightness. The conventional wisdom calls for one light directly on the work surface coming from the side opposite your writing hand. This is supplemented by another fixture providing indirect, or surround lighting, to decrease glare. What I've found is with walls and worktable of light colors or white, enough of the direct illumination gets bounced around to provide the needed indirect light.

Zone Lighting ②. Once you are liberated from the *willy-nilly* illumination of a central fixture, you're free to create several distinct "islands" of light in a single room. You might use low wattage lights or a dimmer in a conversation area. The focus of the dining area is food. Light directed down on the center of the table will also reflect well on the assembled diners. Other zones to consider for special lighting attention: stereo; bookshelves; aquarium.

Mood Lighting ③. You can't do much better than the warm, flickering glow from a wood fire; but candles come close. It's also possible to create some relaxing, unfocused effects with low wattage electric light.

This fixture aimed at light-colored ceiling or wall

A. Direct lighting by Luxo lamp (see p. 64). Added light from hanging fixture.
B. Direct and indirect lighting with track lights (see p. 66.)
C. Direct and supplemental lighting with hanging fixtures. (See p. 63.)

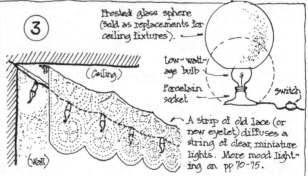

Frosted glass sphere (sold as replacements for ceiling fixtures).

(Ceiling)

(Wall)

Low-wattage bulb

Porcelain socket

switch

A strip of old lace (or new eyelet) diffuses a string of clear, miniature lights. More mood lighting on pp 70-75.

Hangers

Most ceilings are simply walls, tipped sideways. And that's why wall fasteners will also work in ceilings. Here are the ones that will. For more details on each fastener, refer to "On and Off the Wall," pp. 30–45.

The most common ceiling is made just like a hollow wall – regularly spaced 2 x 4s (in ceilings, they're called **joists**, and they're sometimes 2 x 6s or 2 x 8s) covered with gypsum board or, in older places, lath and plaster. Here too, the strongest connection is made by screwing directly into a joist, and drilling is the most reliable way to find one ①. See also the discussion of stud-finding on p. 38.

Where finding studs is difficult, or their location is not just right, you need a fastener that will go through the plaster or gypsum board and spread out on the other side. The choices, in order of increasing strength, are *Togglers*, *Mollys*, and toggle bolts. Since lamps, plants, and other things you suspend from ceilings are often considerably heavier than wall hangings, you need to choose fasteners accordingly ②.

Solid plaster and concrete ceilings are not so common, but they exist, and can be dealt with. The fasteners for hanging are the same ones that were previously prescribed for walls of the same materials ③.

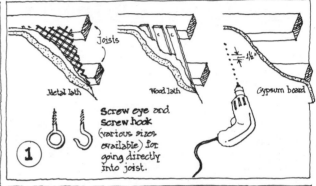

Joists

Metal lath   Wood lath   Gypsum board

Screw eye and screw hook (various sizes available) for going directly into joist.

①

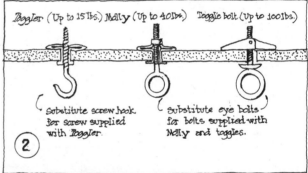

Toggler (Up to 15 lbs.)   *Molly* (Up to 40 lbs.)   Toggle bolt (Up to 100 lbs.)

Substitute screw hook for screw supplied with *Toggler*.

Substitute eye bolts for bolts supplied with *Molly* and toggles.

②

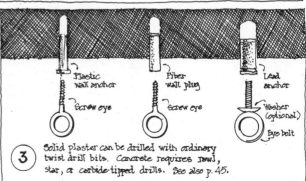

Plastic wall anchor   Fiber wall plug   Lead anchor

Screw eye   Screw eye   Washer (optional)

Eye bolt

③ Solid plaster can be drilled with ordinary twist drill bits. Concrete requires rawl, star, or carbide-tipped drills. See also p. 45.

THE SPIDER CONNECTION:

Wall switch
Controls all lights.

1. Grab your screw-driver and go after mood-destroying central ceiling lights. Here's how to remove the fixture and convert the outlet to a switched power source for lights throughout the room.

2. Start by turning the ceiling fixture on. Then ask a reliable friend to keep an eye on the light while you rummage about pulling fuses (or circuit breakers) one-by-one, until your accomplice yells, "it's off!" or "voilà!" or something appropriate.

3. Now, with the correct circuit turned off, you can remove the old fixture:

Glass bowl
Knurled nut

4. Remove the two screws holding the fixture to the ceiling. Loosen the screws holding the wires to the old fixture. (Some will have wire nut connectors instead of screws. These are simply twisted off.)

Wire Nut

5.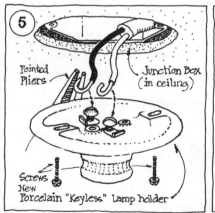

Pointed Pliers

Junction Box (in ceiling)

Screws
New Porcelain "Keyless" Lamp holder

6. Strip ¾" of insulation from each wire. With pointed pliers, (see 5) make a clockwise loop in each. Mount wires under screw heads (black to brass, white to silver) and tighten. Secure lamp holder to junction box with screws supplied.

7 Screw a lamp socket extension into the lamp holder, and a bulb tap into that. Then assemble your hanging lamps. If you're using pulleys, remember to thread them on the wire before putting plugs on.

"Ivory" Plastic Socket Extension

Bulb Tap

8 Cords that support weight must have strain relief:

"Underwriter's Knot" won't pull through plug, or socket casing.

Washer
Screw eye
"S" hook
Aluminum pulley

All the parts shown here are standard hardware store items.

Lamp socket
Shade holder
Sheet metal lampshade (can be spray-painted).

9 Another caution:

(3 oz. lead sinker)

Try to route cords away from main traffic areas, so that dangling pulleys from raised lamps will not damage moving noggins.

Author. (Note multiple scalp wounds.)

10 Tip: To make plugs fit snugly, remove plug from socket, bend prongs outward slightly, then test for fit.

11 This is a "pool" of light. It's much more pleasing to the eye and flattering to the person than illumination that spills all over the place.

12 Note: More than likely you'll be reinstalling that ceiling fixture when you move on. So, before you lose any of the parts, tape them together, label them, (e.g. "living room ceiling") and put them with your ready-to-move stuff. (See also "Better Boxes" p.142.)

Some other shades, and accessories:

Nylon cord supports extra weight of this shade. Once cord is tied, pulley becomes nonfunctional.

Fluted glass Victorian Shade. Watch for these at second-hand stores.

Porcelain enamel shade.

Bare filament bulb looks good in this.

Sta-Tite plug has clean look; tight fit.

An industrial-type plug with handy cord clamp.

Replace the wall switch with an inexpensive dimmer ~ Presto! You have variable control of all the lights on the system, (See p. 73).

UP FRONT LIGHTS

It was playwright Bertold Brecht, or so the story goes, who first decreed that theatrical lights be placed in full view of the audience. This radical idea was meant to undress the illusion of stagecraft and shock the viewers out of their unquestioning emotional response to the play. It didn't work. Audiences continued to suspend disbelief, and Brecht's revolt against style eventually won acceptance as a style of its own. The humble, hard-working industrial light fixture is looking more and more like a piece of sculpture.

This doesn't mean you need smoking, 200-pound Klieg lights in your living room to be counted in the avant-garde. The benefits of portable, flexible, functionally designed lighting can also be had in a scale and degree of refinement you can really live with.

(This is too much.)

Originating in Sweden, this full-floating lamp has been copied many times over. Most of the imitations are not as sturdy as the original, but where a genuine *Luxo* will set you back about $40, a serviceable copy like the *Ledu Econo Lamp* is around $20. I've had four *Ledus* for as many years with only one failure: A pressure adjusting knob got its plastic threads stripped from overzealous tightening. (*Luxos* = all-metal parts.)

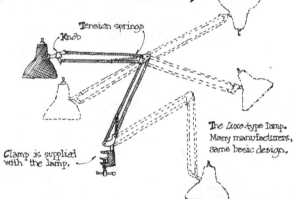

Tension springs

Knob

Clamp is supplied with the lamp.

The *Luxo*-type lamp. Many manufacturers, same basic design.

Picture a lamp moving anywhere within a six-foot sphere and you get an idea of the range of these floating light sources. They are obviously useful for work and study tables, and they're equally at home clamped to a night table for reading in bed. Or arching over an easy chair as an alternative to a table lamp. Turn the shade to face the ceiling, or onto a plant in a corner to make instant ambient lighting. Change the color of the whole room by bringing the lamp close enough to reflect from an intense-hued pillow or wall hanging.

Luxo lamps gain additional flexibility from the assortment of bases and brackets available. There's a weighted stand ③A that turns a *Luxo* into a floor lamp. And a shorter weighted base ③B lets you put a lamp on a piano, a glass table, or other places the standard clamp won't work. There's also a bracket ③c that can be screwed to a wall, a window frame, or the side of a bookcase. ③D is for mounting on horizontal surfaces. ③E and F are clamp-on brackets; the latter allows leveling the lamp on a slanted surface.

Buying and installing extra brackets promotes easy circulation of lamps to different locations. This means that, without buying extra fixtures, you can have good light wherever you (occasionally) need it. I find it helpful to have a bracket near the stereo system for periodic repairs and cleaning.

Contemporary furniture stores usually carry *Luxo* or a similar brand. Also try artist's materials and office supply stores where sales and discounts are more frequent. *Allied Radio* has a kit version of a *Luxo* type lamp for about $12. Wherever you buy your lamps, consider keeping the packing cartons for future damage-free moving.

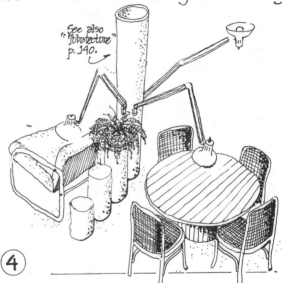

See also "Tubotecture" p. 140.

Clamp lamps are not as flexible, nor as stylish as *Luxos*. They're also one-eighth to one-fourth the cost. This is the standard hardware store item: a rubber padded spring clamp mounted to a swivel-socket and then to a porcelain lamp base. A spot or flood lamp with

Clamp Lamp

built-in reflector is all you need to complete the basic fixture. It can be clamped to a shelf, to the headboard of a bed, or to the top of a framed mirror.

A clamp lamp is also a good temporary solution to positioning a sun or heat lamp. (Because of dangerous heat build-up don't use reflectors with these bulbs.) For more permanent installations, I have removed the spring clamp and used the ball and socket hardware alone. It makes a neat connection, for example, to the top of a music stand.

Hardware store clamp lamps may be the height of function, but that doesn't mean you'll find them easy to look at. Fortunately, some enterprising designers and manufacturers — spotting a good idea — have added a bit of fashion to the clamp lamp without sacrificing any of the function. Here are a couple of examples:

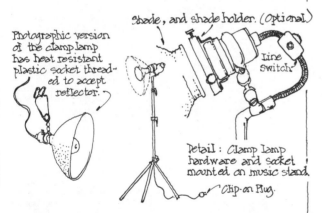

C2 clip spot. Chrome, white or brown. About $24 each. From Conran's, N.Y.

Shade available in white or chocolate — sold only in pairs: 19.95. J.C. Penney or Sears.

Photographic version of the clamp lamp has heat resistant plastic socket threaded to accept reflector.

Shade, and shade holder. (Optional.)

Line Switch.

Detail: Clamp lamp hardware and socket mounted on music stand.

or Clip-on Plug.

Track Lighting. Industry, not the theatre, is the original source for continuous bus bar-like channels with snap-in light fixtures. Track lighting, as the system is now called, went through its first metamorphosis to become flexible fixtures for store displays. Additional refinement, and an explosion of styles and accessories, accompanied its introduction to the home lighting market.

The idea has really been overpromoted for home use, and many miles of track have been expensively installed where one or two ordinary fixtures were all that was needed. For renters, though, who must repeatedly deal with

After cutting off the molded plug, thread the wire through the telescoping tubes of the stand, then install a clip-on plug. An in-line switch completes this industrial-look, lightweight, folding floor lamp.

new and mostly ill-lit rooms, track lighting is worth considering.

All of the different track lighting systems share some common features. The track itself is usually an extruded aluminum channel which looks something like this:

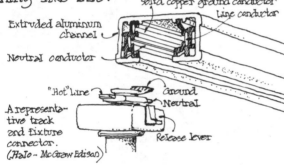

Extruded aluminum channel

Neutral conductor

solid copper ground conductor

Line conductor

"Hot" Line

Ground

Neutral

A representative track and fixture connector. (Halo - McGraw Edison)

Release lever

Each lamp fixture has prongs which make contact with the copper "rails" of the track when they are inserted and given a quarter-turn. That's the basic mechanics of it. Beyond that, the changes that can be rung are almost endless. Fixtures come in spheres, rectangles, and cylinders. With combinations of fixtures, bulbs, and lenses you can throw a high intensity spotlight on a flowering plant; project a perfectly focused rectangle of light on a framed picture; or "wash" a whole wall with even illumination. From at least one company, *Lightolier*, you can even get a slick-looking fluorescent fixture that plugs into their *Lytespan* track.

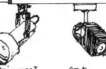

Universal (by Halo ~ $36 *)

Spot (Prescolight ~ $26)

Wall-washer (Halo ~ $56.)

Framing Projector (Swivelier ~ $26.)

Installation of track lighting ranges from plug-in simplicity to semi-permanent complexity. The usual method is to surface mount the track with one end overlapping a ceiling outlet box. A specially-designed canopy and "live end" feed power from the outlet to the track. The track itself (2, 4, 8, and 12 feet are standard lengths) can be mounted to the ceiling with toggle or Molly bolts. Mark the positions for these by slipping the track onto the live end after it has been fastened to the canopy. (Current is off, of course!) *Lightolier's Lytespan* track has special clips that can be pre-mounted to the ceiling. The track is then mounted to the clips.

Ceiling outlet

Cover

Canopy

Live end

Cover

Making it simple. Almost all track lighting manufacturers make an accessory that replaces the live end with

* Approximate *List* Prices. Contractors and Architects commonly get 40% off. Try to become friendly with one.
Track length shown, 4 feet, about $22. Track and fixtures by *different* manufacturers are *not* compatible.

a cord and plug. This makes installation far less permanent and also
allows for mounting the track up to
12 feet (the length of cord and plug)
from the nearest outlet box.

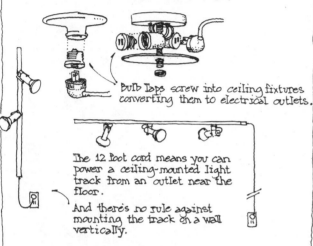

Bulb Taps screw into ceiling fixtures
converting them to electrical outlets.

The 12 foot cord means you can
power a ceiling-mounted light
track from an outlet near the
floor.

And there's no rule against
mounting the track on a wall
vertically.

Here are some other accessories that
add to track lighting versatility:

Outlet Adapter.
Lets you tap
into track and
power any fixture
with a 3-prong
plug.

Pendant Adapter.
Allows any chain-
hung fixture (up
to 35 pounds) to
be suspended from
track.

"L" Connector.
To turn a corner
with track.

Straight Connector.
For connecting two
tracks end-to-end.
("T" and "X" connectors
are also available.)

C-Clamp Adapter (Halo).
Mounts on 2 inch pipe
(or 1 inch board)
Six foot cord and plug.
Accepts any track
fixture.

An unusual track lighting system with
no live conductors is offered by
Conran's (the New York transplant of
London's innovative *Habitat* stores).
The fixtures slide anywhere along an
all-plastic track. Power is supplied
through expanding, telephone-type
cords with a clip-together plug arrangement. Two styles of spot lights
can be ordered, and there's an extra
outlet in the track to feed a drop
light.

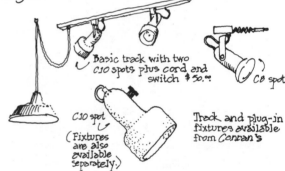

Basic track with two
C10 spots plus cord and
switch $50.⁰⁰

C8 spot

C10 spot
(Fixtures
are also
available
separately.)

Track and plug-in
fixtures available
from Conran's

Making your own tracks. Some of the
same versatility of commercial track
lighting is possible at less than one-
fourth the cost in a home-made
version.

The lights are fixed along the length
of the "track" but swivel sockets permit
aiming them in virtually any direction.
This system is a natural for turning
a hallway into a picture gallery.
You can adjust the length of the "track"
and the number of fixtures to cus-

tom fit your own situation. And by suspending the whole unit 6 to 12 inches below the hall ceiling you can add some sculptural interest to an ordinarily sterile space.

Ceiling fixture can be tapped for power (see p. 62.) or simply run the cord down the wall to an outlet.

1"x6" board

Porcelain Socket.

Swivel Socket.

Flood or spot lamp with built-in reflector.

Swivel Sockets. Two of several different styles are illustrated. The one on the right is about $4.00. The other is about a dollar more.

Back view of 1" by 6" showing how porcelain socket is mounted. Opening is made with hole saw. Carefully slit lamp cord and divide along seam. Strip one inch of insulation from each conductor and wrap around terminal screws. Continue cord to next socket and repeat this procedure.

Off the track. In a short hall or entryway you may want the aiming and focusing features of track lighting, but minus the track. Most track lighting makers have foreseen this possibility and offer versions of their track fixtures designed for direct mounting to any outlet box.

Direct mounting fixture... ... Halo

Just inside the front door of my house there's a shallow built-in bookcase. It's the first thing you see when you enter. I removed the ceiling fixture (putting a merciful end to its fatuous impersonation of an antique carriage lantern) and replaced it with a *Lightolier* fixture. The result is dramatic. Concentrated light makes everyone who enters focus in on the display of tin toys in the bookcase. It's a real crowd pleaser.

Ceiling outlet box

75w. spot

Wire nuts

Drilled hole

Lamp cord to outlet

In a previous rental, I mounted the same fixture on a wall where there was no outlet box. The only modification was drilling a hole in the side of the canopy base and connecting a lamp cord and plug with wire nuts.

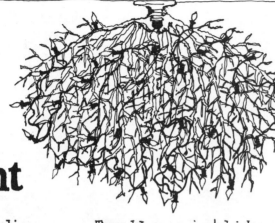

Light Delight

Organic Chandelier. Here is maximum elegance with minimum expense and effort. Just weave one string of all-white miniature lamps into a dried, and sun-bleached tumbleweed. Use a pipe cleaner to wrap around a ceiling outlet and the "trunk" of the bush.

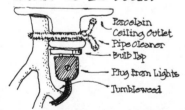

Porcelain Ceiling Outlet
Pipe Cleaner
Bulb Tap
Plug from Lights
Tumbleweed

Plug in the lights, and you have a startlingly original light fixture to shed a soft glow over a dining table. Where do you get tumbleweeds?

They blow against highway fences throughout the Southwest. If you're nowhere near there, substitute dried branches trimmed from privet or other hedges or even from an oak tree. Whatever you use, take the precaution of spraying thoroughly with the fire retardant also used for Christmas trees. In the off-season, miniature Christmas tree lights are available at store decorators' supply houses.

Socket Octopus. Take one rather mundane piece of industrial hardware, and multiply it over and over and it turns into something else. It may be humorous, it may even be art. Take the lowly duplex bulb socket for example.

Duplex Socket Extension ~ About $1.00

All by itself it's functional, but no great shakes on the aesthetic plane. Yet, put a dozen or so of these together, so that they take on the appearance of overgrown plastic coral, put seven-watt clear bulbs in the open ends, and look again. Is it art? Or is it only funny looking?

Light Beer. Like the other suggestions here, these bottled lights aspire to beauty rather than function. And of course, the better-looking the bottles the better-looking the lamp. *Carlsberg Malt Liquor*, *Grolsch*, and *Watney's* are a few brews that I

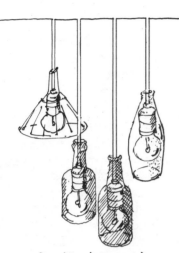

This spun aluminum shade is made to screw directly onto a metal socket.

switch

(About $6.00 at photo supply stores.)

know of with interesting bottle shapes and colors. But you may want to do your own in-depth research on this. You'll also need to borrow a bottle-cutter (unless you were one of the millions who got them as ecological Christmas gifts). Cut the bottom off the bottles and thread them over a lamp cord on which you've put a metal or porcelain lamp socket. Be sure and tie a stress-relieving "Underwriter's knot" in the cord (see page 63). Wire your lamps (they look best in groups) to a ceiling fixture or add plugs and switches and run the cords to a wall outlet.

Tree Lamp. Why not sit under a tree to read your evening newspaper—especially if the light is good and there aren't any mosquitoes? Such a bucolic setting only requires a comfortable chair and the corner of one room, plus a selected, full-of-character dead tree branch. But make sure the branch is truly dead. Some are homes for future generations of wood-eating insects. A dead branch pruned from an otherwise healthy tree should be okay. Driftwood branches are good-looking and usually inert.

Mount your specimen on a base cut from scrap lumber. An octagon is an easy-to-cut and appropriate shape. Two 3 to 4-inch lag screws will hold an average limb, and make removal of the base possible.

If you nail 3 glides into the bottom of the base it will sit level and the lag screw heads won't need to be countersunk:

Branch

Furniture glides

Lag screws

Selected river rocks give the base extra weight and stability. The lamp cord can't be hidden, so make it part of the design. Use white or clear cord, thread it through screw eyes (snug fit) and stretch it taut. A switch on the socket controls off/on; or install a line switch, or small dimmer on the cord.

Tin Can Twilight. The most appealing, room-changing light I've ever seen, issued from an empty five-gallon olive oil can. I was renting a houseboat at the time, subletting at first from a musician. Since his own next landing place was uncertain, he temporarily bequeathed me his collection of 300 records,* and his psychedelic approach to floating-home decoration. The tin-can lamp was part of the deal, but it transcended all the rest. An arabesque of thousands of tiny holes had been meticulously punched in the sides of the can by someone with the patience of a monk.

Five gallon olive oil tin (from a restaurant).

Clear 25 w. bulb
Porcelain socket
Wood block

Inside the bottom-up can was a single, clear 25 watt bulb, providing the necessary point source of light. The effect with all other lights out, was magical. Each hole projected a tiny beam of light. The walls and ceilings were covered with stars. Since then I've discovered a plan for making a smaller version of this tin can lantern. It's a little less ambitious and just about as dazzling.

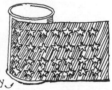

Draw (or find) a pattern to guide the hole punching. Gift wrap paper is a possibility.

Use an empty quart size juice can. Fill it with water and put it in the freezer for a day or two. When it's frozen solid, remove, and using gloves, a hammer, an awl or sharp nail, punch a decorative pattern of holes all around the can. (The ice inside supports the can so it doesn't buckle under the blows.)

Artificial Heavens. I guess I was inspired by that lamp to be very conscious of the other lighting in my tiny ark. Or it could have been that in that essentially one-room space, nothing much _could_ change except the lighting. I couldn't move into a different room, so I would turn off the light over the sink and turn on the light over the dining table. Like theater-in-the-round, there were no scene changes — just a change of emphasis.

Lighting played an important role in the slightly separate bedroom, too. Here a Captain's bunk filled one end of the tiny space. Wooden columns and carved frieze completed the enclosure. It was all warmth and invitation until you crawled in and looked up at the blank ceiling. Soo...

Using an old lace tablecloth (yup — it's the same one that's resurrected on

* Thanks, Jim, wherever you are ... and I'm sorry about the mirror, really.

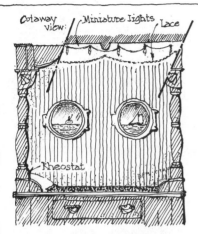

Cutaway view: Miniature lights Lace

Rheostat

p. 57). I lowered the visual ceiling inside the area bounded by the bed. Then in the space between the lace and the original ceiling I strung miniature Christmas tree lights, spaced at regular intervals and stapled* to the ceiling. The lights were plugged into an extension cord equipped with a small dimmer. With the lace in position, the lights and wires were invisible. Imagine the effect, then, lying in the bed at dusk, staring up at the pattern of lace and slowly little multi-colored stars come out of the dark.

Lowlights. The lights slowly dim in the great hall. An expectant hush comes over the crowd. What power! For a moment a single person with a rheostat has God-like authority. What a draw for a smallish boy with dreams of glory and no athletic prowess. I joined the stage crew because the high school auditorium had the biggest bank of shiny black rheostats I had ever seen. Much later (but not yet into the era of transistor-equipped matchbox-size dimmers) I built my own light control station from a hulking, war-surplus rheostat.

The surplus, labor-intensive dimmer.   The $5.98 off-the-shelf item.

Now you can buy rheostats in supermarkets that work better and cost less than my home-made monstrosity.

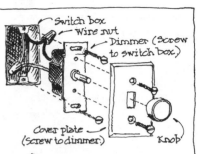

Switch box
Wire nut
Dimmer (screw to switch box.)
Cover plate (screw to dimmer)   Knob

The $5.98 model is designed to replace a wall switch. Then whatever that switch controls (ceiling fixture; wall outlets) will be controlled by the dimmer. Note: Take some care in connecting wall outlets to a dimmer. It's a good idea to label these so you (or someone else) doesn't plug in something the dimmer can't tolerate: fluorescents, appliances, TVs, radios, and/or anything that uses more than 600 watts of power. (Some dimmers will handle more power — check the rating printed on the packaging or stamped into the device.)

Dimmer installation. First, locate the breaker panel or fuse box (usually near the electric meter). Turn off all power. Re-

---

★ Use fence staples, tapped in (Staple) (Wire) with a tack hammer. Do <u>not</u> use a staple gun!

move the old switch and disconnect the wires. Connect the dimmer to the same wires that went to the switch. Leave the other wires undisturbed.

Now screw the dimmer to the wall box, screw the cover plate to the dimmer and slide on the knob. (Turn to p.73 to see a whole system of lights you can control from a single dimmer.)

Mini-Dimmers. Add a few dollars to what you'd pay for a built-in dimmer, and get one you can install directly on a lamp cord. Advantages: quick installation and the ability to put a switch/dimmer exactly where you want it. (Control bedroom lights with a switch beside the bed!) Disadvantages: Initial cost and limited capacity (typically 200 watts). It's tempting to mount the dimmer on an extension cord, so that you can easily

connect various combinations of lamps to it. That's fine; but I know from experience it's easy to exceed 200 watts and zip — there goes your eight-dollar dimmer.

Control knob. In this *Leviton* model, turning the knob counterclockwise all the way switches power off.

Mini-Dimmer Installation. First, make sure the lamp cord is not plugged in. Then, with a sharp knife, slice between the two strands of the cord without cutting the insulation. Separate the wires for about 2½ inches, and cut one of the strands in the middle of this opening.

Strip about ¾ inch of insulation from each cut end. Remove the cover and thread the wire through the dimmer, stuffing the uncut strand down into the shell and fastening the exposed wires under the two terminal screws.

Attach the cord to a lamp (or lamps) of known wattage and plug it in.

Part of the cost of dimmers can be offset by the savings in electricity, and especially in extra bulb life. (A five per cent reduction in power <u>doubles</u> bulb-life expectancy.)

Solid state lamp dimmer

This is another compact dimmer. This one puts control right at the lightbulb. It's obviously aimed at tablelamps, but you may come up with another use.

A very simple dinner party I once attended had some memorable lighting. The room lights were turned way down and every table setting had its own candle. This elegance was also affordable, because small votive candles (about 65 cents for eight ten-hour candles) were simply set in baby-food jars.

Another small-effort, big payoff candle trick is to put them in rooms where your decorating scheme has not quite come together. I've made a half-finished bathroom look presentable for parties by turning off the lights and leaving only a couple of candles burning. Use lightly scented candles and you have a very deceptively inviting room.

A superior candle. Since inexpensive candles use petroleum-based paraffin, and natural beeswax is out of sight, its nice to know about Flam'buoy-ants. First, because they burn only salad oil (a plant-based renewable resource) and second, because they are very clever and good-looking. For about two dollars you get a small box containing three clear plastic "buoys" and a hundred (or so) special wicks. You provide a drinking glass, plain or fancy, filled to within one inch of the rim with water, and topped off with ½ inch of any salad oil.

Wick — Floating buoy
½" oil
Water

Put a wick in the buoy, drop the buoy onto the oil and light. They will burn for hours with nary a drip or sputter. And if this leads you to forget them, they will extinguish themselves when the oil is gone.

The buoys can be washed with detergent and water and reused indefinitely. Flam'buoy-ants come with complete instructions and are unconditionally guaranteed. Just don't get experimental: kerosene, animal fats, and scented lamp oils are potentially dangerous substitutions. Stick with vegetable oil.

Invert a Japanese paper umbrella, trim the handle and tape or wire to the overhead fixture. (A dimestore or photo umbrella will also work.)

Bill Wells reminds me that some people may find ceiling fixtures not as repugnant as I do, and suggests an inverted umbrella as a light softening solution or at the very least a temporary stop-gap.

75

3
Openings

Doors and windows are openings—holes in our spaces that are as important as the openings in our faces. Through the door I can see that *other* room; and so I'm more aware of being in *this* one. A glance at the window reminds me that I am inside looking out.

Imagine yourself at age ten. You are trick-or-treating on Halloween night. You come to the house or apartment where you live now. Look it over and decide whether you feel comfortable enough to walk up and ring the doorbell.

Openings can also be *un*inviting, without giving offense. A sign on my son's door says "Jordy's Room." It reminds me that under some circumstances I may be intruding.

Windows are our contact with the real world. Through them comes the daylight that may be essential to our health, both physical and spiritual. Plants thrive in windows, reminding us of our own biological links to what's beyond the glass.

Windows have an additional life-enhancing role. They give and take energy. It flows out, of course, when they're open; but even a tightly-closed window spills heat faster than a wall. So curtains and blinds put up to change the light may also, if designed for it, restrict the loss of energy.

Windows also admit the warming sun, and provide heat-gain during the day. When heat absorbing masses are in the sun's path they collect and then give back at night what they've gathered all day.

Windows and doors are interruptions. They are active and attract attention. Ever notice how people find so much to say while standing in doorways? Concentrate your improvements on doors and windows and you multiply the impact. Just as a little eye shadow or a mustache can have a big effect on a face, small changes around the openings of your rooms can work wonders.

WINDOW ME-CHANICS

A little inside knowledge, a little probing under the skin of things, can bring extra understanding and creativity to a simple task. So before you start dressing your windows, do some imaginary undressing. Take this skeletal course in window types, how to maintain them, and where to attach things to them.

Double-hung windows. Traditionally made of wood, this design ① goes back hundreds of years. Abandoned in the '50's in favor of more easily maintained aluminum sash, wood double-hung windows are now making a comeback because of their better appearance and greater insulation val-

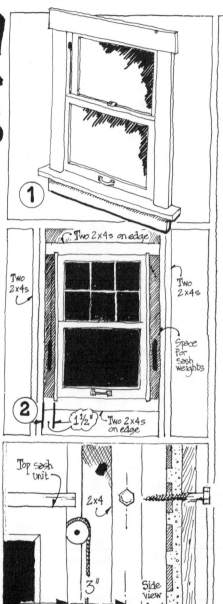

Two 2x4s on edge

Two 2x4s

Two 2x4s

Space for sash weights

1½" Two 2x4s on edge

Top sash unit

2x4

3"

Side view

ues. They're superior in another way, too. You can attach light-weight curtain rods, and window shade brackets directly to the wide wooden trim pieces that usually surround these windows. Heavier items need to be attached to something more substantial though. This means finding the structural framing of the window, which, if you had x-ray eyes, would look something like ②. Note the extra space between the side jamb and the vertical 2x4s. This is the <u>window pocket</u> for the sash weights, the suspended, counterbalancing lead weights which give double-hung windows their name.

Measuring out three inches ③ should get you safely to the middle of the first of these 2x4s. Of course, whatever you're hoping will take hold in the

78

2x4 must run through the trim, through the plasterboard, and <u>then</u> into the 2x4 ③.

Double-hung detailing.

If you're lucky enough to have wooden windows, you probably won't want to hide them. Two simple operations can make a vast improvement in their looks — scraping and cleaning. Scraping is to correct the legacy of sloppiness from previous paint jobs ④. A good, close scraping job requires several blade changes, so I suggest getting a scraper that takes ordinary single-edge razor blades rather than expensive special blades. Basic technique is to keep a shallow angle to the glass and after peeling up several inches of paint, turn the blade 90 degrees and run it back over the edge just scraped to cut the lifted paint cleanly away.

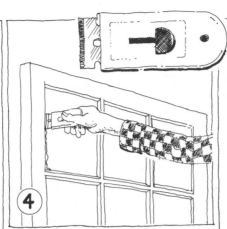

Another advantage of double-hung windows is that the outside of the glass can be cleaned from inside the building ⑤. But this depends on your having both upper and lower sash moveable. Since the top sash is little-used, it is often glued shut by several coats of paint. A wide putty knife tapped gently into the seam where sash meets parting strip should crack it open and make it usable ⑥. The outside may need the same treatment, but for this you'll probably need a ladder. From outside you can also use a thin pry bar over the top of the upper sash to gently encourage movement ⑥. To prevent future sticking, remove any traces of paint from the channels with a sharp chisel and/or fine sandpaper wrapped around a block of wood. Dust, and then use a paraffin block,

79

beeswax, or a bar of hard soap to lubricate the channel.

Casement windows

① with frames of wood, aluminum, or steel, are the second most widely used type. This group includes all windows made to hinge on one vertical edge and swing open, like a door. Casement windows don't have sash weights and that means no voids in the window framing... the 2 x 4s are right there, next to the edges of the window frame, covered only with plasterboard and, rarely, a narrow wood trim strip ①.

Casement Cleanup.

Casement windows have few maintenance requirements. A recalcitrant crank is the most likely complaint. And a simple cleaning and oiling of the crank handle is the almost sure-fire solution.

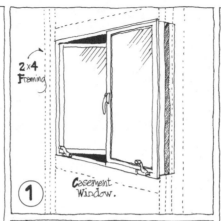

2 x 4 Framing

① Casement Window.

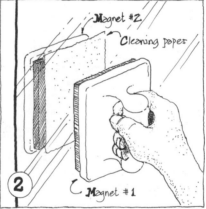

Magnet #2
Cleaning paper
② Magnet #1

③ Sliding Window

Newer model casement windows are made so that the hinged side swings toward the center of the opening as the other side swings out. This means that both sides of the glass can be cleaned from inside. Older, fixed-hinge casements are a different story: You clean the outside from the outside. But there's something better on the way. It's the *Magna Clean* window washer and it's made to clean the outside of the glass from the inside ②. Even fixed glass can be cleaned if any part of it can be reached from a nearby opening. Half of the magnetized cleaning platen must be stuck on the outside of the window opposite its magnetic mate (also the handle) on the inside.

Sliding Windows ③

made either of wood or aluminum are a third, far less common type. Rough framing is similar to casement windows; the 2×4s will be right next to the outside perimeter of the window, allowing only for the thickness of plasterboard or wood trim ③.

Consider a wood slider to be a double-hung window on its side. Clean and wax or soap the sliding parts, especially the lower track, which, being horizontal, is a real dirt magnet. Aluminum sliders also need frequent track cleaning (a narrow vacuum cleaner wand gets the crevices). Spraying silicone lubricant on all sliding parts is the crowning touch.

Awning and **jalousie** **windows** show up in some places ④. Basic maintenance is lubrication of moving parts. Framing is just the same as for casement and sliding windows.

Awning

Jalousie

④

Vinyl tube insulation comes in coils. Use non-rusting nails to install.

A.

⑤ B.

Use adhesive-backed foam strips for casement or awning-type windows.

⑥

Transparent vinyl tape is some help for jalousies.

Window Insulation.

Penetration, the movement of air through openings in the outside walls of your rented rooms, accounts for nearly half the heat lost from the structure. And poorly fitting windows account for most of these openings. So here is one case where the temporary resident can do something substantial to save energy and also be around to reap the reward in lowered utility costs. The materials and time needed to plug leaks around windows are modest, the job can be done a little at a time, and each increment will help.

Illustration ⑤ shows vinyl tube insulation installed under the bottom rail of the upper sash, **A** and on the parting strip and the bottom rail of the lower sash, **B**. Illustration ⑥ covers casement, awning and jalousie types. ✍

81

Quick Covers

Not too long after you move into your new apartment, you're going to become aware of the view. I don't mean what you see when you look out the windows. I mean what the neighbors see when they look <u>in</u>.

Unless you harbor some latency as a flasher, or a bathtub-to-bedroom streaker, you've probably already resorted to some expedient... like Indian bedspreads held in place with thumbtacks.

When you're ready for a bit more refinement, here are some ways to have it, without a whole lot of work. One easy step up from Indian bedspreads is the push-pin-pleat method of curtain hanging ①.

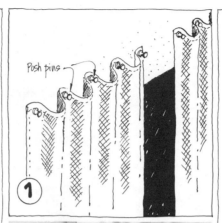

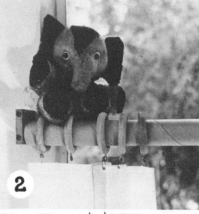

Push pins

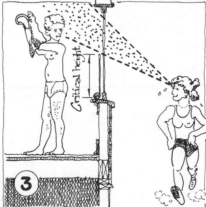

Critical height

Measure and cut two panels of fabric, four to eight inches longer than the window, and almost as wide. Muslin, denim, eyelet, lace, and corduroy — just about any straight-hanging fabric will do. Hem the top, bottom, and sides by turning under an inch of the material and sewing, gluing, or ironing on mending tape. (Use the selvage as a hem wherever you can.)

Next, get about 20 push pins (or thumbtacks — or even a stapler will do) and starting at one corner of the fabric, pin and pleat your way across the top of the window (easier to draw than to describe... see ①). Be prepared to go back and adjust the pleats once or twice before you get it just right.

Very often, it's just the lower half of a window that needs to be screened. Most potential *look-ers* are below the level of the window, and most *Jookees* are only modest from the armpits down. Thus, critical lines of sight are established as diagrammed in ③.

Now, if you determine that half a curtain is better than one, here's an easy way to do it ④. Just drive two nails (or use brass screws for more finesse) into the sides of the window at the top of your proposed curtain. Wrap bare copper or brass wire around one nail, then stretch it across to the other. Allow an extra couple of inches and cut the wire. Measure and cut two curtain panels leaving about 2½ inches extra at the top for the sleeve. Sew, glue, or tape the sleeve and hems, and thread the wire through the sleeves of both panels. Stretch the wire taut and wrap the free end around the nail (or screw).

The next design is some-

"shirred" effect comes from fabric being about twice the actual width of the opening.

④

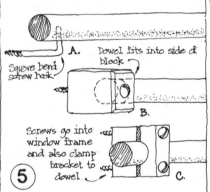

A. Dowel fits into side of block
Square bend screw hook
B.
Screws go into window frame and also clamp bracket to dowel
⑤
C.

Wood curtain rings
Dowel
Screw eye
Safety pin.

⑥

what more complicated, but it looks good and it travels well. To start, you'll need a ¾ to 1 inch dowel, two to four inches wider than the window frame, and about 12 2¾ inch wooden curtain rings. (a hardware or fabric store item). Support the dowel in one of the ways shown in ⑤.

Next, measure, cut, and hem two curtain panels, making each panel twice the final width to allow for pleats. (Note that this method will work for half or full-length curtains. To make a pleat, fold the hemmed edge of the curtain as shown ⑥ and secure to the screw eye in the curtain ring with a small brass safety pin. Expect some trial and error in getting the pleats even.

Slide the completed curtains onto the dowel and mount the brackets on the window. ✿

Out·of·Sight Windows

I've spent a lot of time around "media people": photographers, filmmakers, television people. They are, as a group, very pale. I wonder if, through natural selection perhaps, certain mole-like individuals end up in these window-less jobs? Or do they simply put up with all-day darkness because of other inducements? I don't know... for them. For me, this occupational hazard had a sizable influence on my decision to move away from film production into writing and illustrating. Now I get to work in front of a window and even look up occasionally. Still, the need to darken a room for film and slide projection means that I've at least got to have convertible windows. Here's one solution ①. When this rigid blind is up, not a photon of light is blocked, but when it's down there's a complete blackout. If the room geometry permits, a projection screen can be mounted right on the blind. A sheet of silvered *Mylar* on the other side will reflect the sun's heat when the blind is down, and bounce a little extra light into the room when it's up.

"Hinge"

Cloth, wrapped and stapled. (¼" staple)

⅛" *Masonite*, glued and stapled (⁹/₁₆" staples) to artist's stretcher bars — (available from art supply stores).

If *Masonite* is not used, stretcher bars can be glued and stapled at corners (⁹/₁₆" staples). Or use staples only, to keep the frame demountable.

⅛" untempered *Masonite* glued and stapled (⁹/₁₆" staples) to 1 x 2 lumber.

(If *Masonite* is not used, use screws or nails and glue to reinforce corners.)

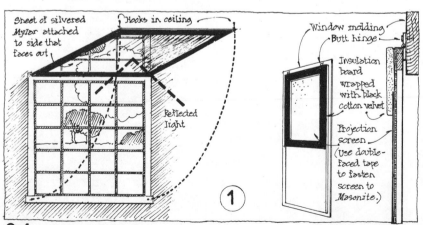

Sheet of silvered *Mylar* attached to side that faces out

Hooks in ceiling

Reflected light

Window molding

Butt hinge

Insulation board wrapped with black cotton velvet

Projection screen (use double-faced tape to fasten screen to *Masonite*.)

①

Now, with just a little more work, and the substitution of some ½ inch insulation board (in place of the *Masonite*) your blind takes on another role as an effective thermal insulator ②. To get the maximum insulating value, run foam adhesive-backed insulating tape around the perimeter of the blind, and put two latches at the bottom to hold it tight against the window casings. Substitute butt hinges for screw eyes to make the top more rigid.

White-out. The same idea can be used to make rigid blinds that let light in, while also working to discourage peeping Toms, block a view of neighbor's garbage cans, disguise an awkward window, and/or cut down a little on the transmission of noise and drafts ③.

Now, if you're handier with a sewing machine than a staple gun, or just want something softer and easier to put away than a rigid blind, take a look at ④. Made with blue denim or black cotton velvet, this also works as a blackout curtain for slide and movie shows.

Note that all of these blinds are measured and cut for specific windows. What about using them in your next rental? It's surprising, but they usually do fit into new places. Sometimes two panels can be sewn together; or the width will be right and only the length needs taking in. Fabric can be removed from rigid panels and the frames recut. I can't remember ever throwing away a piece of window covering. No piece is ever so small it can't at least live again as napkins or a potholder.

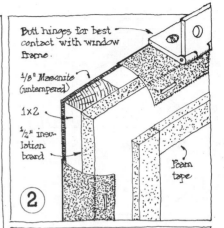

Butt hinges for best contact with window frame.

⅛" Masonite (untempered)

1 x 2

½" insulation board

Foam tape

②

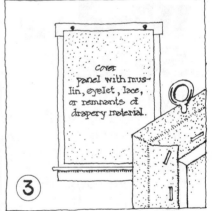

Cover panel with muslin, eyelet, lace, or remnants of drapery material.

③

⅜" dowel in hemmed sleeve.

Stretched fabric

Screw hook

④

Window Settee

My first San Francisco apartment (\$90 per month in 1964) had not one, but two bay windows. Now the view wasn't anything to write home about, but the windows did deliver a lot of light. This is the window seat I built to take advantage of all that brightness. You may not have a bay window, but the design is basic; it can be adapted to many situations.

My bench was made entirely of 2 by 2 inch clear fir. Construction grade fir is an acceptable substitute, especially if your lumber dealer lets you be selective. If the bench is to go into a confined space – a bay window, or a nook – it's wise to cut and trial-fit the 2 by 2s on the floor directly under the window.

Establish the height of the bench – 14 to 18 inches is comfortable for sitting – mark the wall and measure up from this mark about 18 inches, on either side of the center window, to locate the screw eyes, drill pilot holes, and be sure they pass through the window frame into a solid framing member.

Next, cut two 2 by 2s for the cross bars and lay these across the lateral 2 by 2s. The cross bars should be the same distance apart as the screw eyes in the window frame.

Foam Pads

Crate-Construction Boxes, See p. 144

Recessed Base

Some Other Possibilities

Ledger Resting on Baseboard and Attached to Studs

Window Settee in Square Bay

Use nails, screws, or even heavy twine to attach the crossbars at every intersection.

Now turn the bench over and put 3/16 or 1/4 inch eye bolts near the front of the crossbars.

Mount a 2 by 2 ledger on the wall where the back of the bench will rest.

Find studs and use lag screws for maximum strength. Then lift the bench into position, the back resting on the ledger, the front temporarily propped with a stack of books.

Cable and cable clamps stretched between the eye bolts in the bench and the screw eyes in the window frames complete the construction.

The bench can be coated with polyurethane varnish for an impervious-to-just-about-everything finish. Less tough, but softer to the touch, is plastic oil. A light, preliminary wiping with white pigmented wood stain will counteract the darkening effect of subsequent coats of varnish or oil. You can also just leave the wood unfinished. Dirt and grease marks can be removed with a fine grade of sandpaper.

The bench turns out to be a great place for plants; and a few judiciously placed cushions make it equally fine for people. 🐌

WINDOW MUSEUM

Got a lovely view of the neighbor's garbage can? A straight shot of the window in the apartment next door? These pages may help. They're about losing the view without losing the light, and about turning a liability into an asset.

1 If the straight ahead view is no prize, how about bending it? It's done with mirror tiles mounted to a hinged, adjustable board:

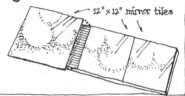

12" x 12" mirror tiles

2

FROM SKY

⅛" wire rope cable clamps

screw eye

A.

steel chain

wood screw

B.

Trial-fit mirror panel to determine best angle. Then lock in place using detail A or B.

Bottom of panel is secured with hinges. Leave space at bottom for water run-off.

3 Stained glass on a beer budget? (Not one, but _two_ ways.) First, a ladder of shelves holding jars of colored water. Jars are accumulated from daily use: peanut butter, mayonnaise, fruit juices, Mason jars, etc.

4

Shelf unit is made from 1" x 6" lumber measured and cut to fit inside the window frame. This means that most of the weight of the shelf and contents will be supported by the window sill. Two nails driven through the bottom shelf into the sill and two brackets screwed to the top complete the fastening. A drop or two of chlorine bleach plus food coloring makes colored water that won't grow algae.

*

* At least one of these two screws must go through the casing into the rough framing.

5 You can get closer to the real effect of stained glass by tinting ordinary glass with window dyes. The materials, sold in craft shops, include compounds you can paint on under the colors to give the texture of old glass.

6 Rather than imitating stained glass, use the dyes as an art form of a different order. And save your creation by doing the work on a separate piece of glass — then hang it in front of the existing window.

7 If your view only needs slight enhancement, consider corner glasses. Make your own with window dyes or convince your local stained-glass artisan of their commercial potential, and take the first few they make in exchange for your brilliant idea.

.... And a tip of the hat to *Abracadabra Stained Glass Windows* who gave *me* the idea.

8 The next device screens the view completely, but turns the light that *is* admitted into a continuous, varied show. The range of possible light transformers is not limited to those shown. Surplus stores, craft stores, and *Edmund Scientific Company* will supply additional inspiration.

A. Crooke's Radiometer spins at up to 3000 rpm in sunlight or when exposed to any infrared radiation, even the glow from a cigarette. About $7.00 from *Edmund Scientific.*

B. *Spectrarc* window-prism. 12" curved triangular bar shapes and focuses a spectrum, all the colors of the rainbow, on the walls and ceiling of your room. About $20.00 from *The Nature Company.*

C. One-way mirror centered on a bird feeder provides undetected close-ups. Transparent mirror film, about $2.50 (10" x 18") from *Edmund Scientific.*

D. Solar converter uses photo-voltaic cell to drive small electric motor. About $12.00 from *Edmund Scientific.*

E. & F. Fresnel lenses. The rectangular sheet reduces your view to a manageable 1¼" x 1½" and repeats it 25 times. The round one gives you a fisheye view of the world outside. About $5.00 each from *Edmund Scientific.*

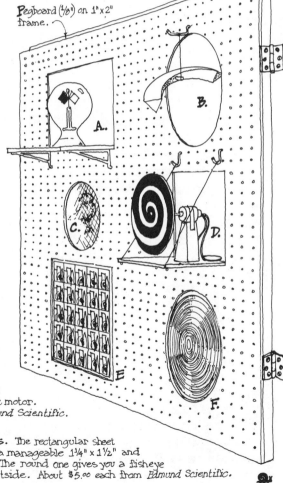

Pegboard (⅛") on 1" x 2" frame.

DOOR LORE

Doors take a beating and usually don't mention it. They survive all the urgencies of animal scratchings, the slammings and bangings of kids, and the vagaries of the weather. On the other hand, nothing calls attention like a door that won't work. A door that sticks or refuses to close invites the danger of theft and possibly impaired fire exits, not to mention the gobs of expensive warmth lost through poorly fitting doors. These are reasons enough not to wait for the owner to get around to fixing your doors.

Door lore has its creative aspects as well. Doors can do more than close openings. They can become part of your furnishings by carrying

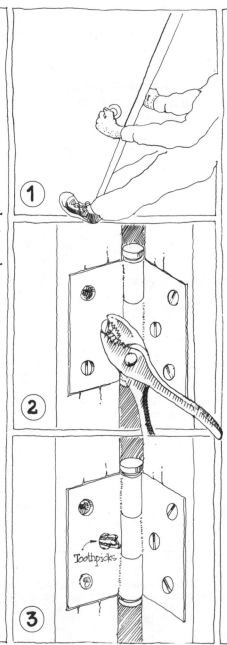

① ② ③ Toothpicks

storage and information, and they can lead other lives as tables. But to make full use of this versatility it's necessary to know what makes doors tick — or rather squeak.

Squeaking / Creaking
A creaking door — the familiar haunted house effect — is the symptom of a hinge that needs oiling. But squeaking is the wood-against-wood sound of a door that's beginning to bind. No use trying to adapt to the sound; it is probably going to get worse. The result: a full-fledged stuck door. The cause of this can be very simple — loose hinges. To test for this open the door and stand facing the latch. Grasp a door knob in each hand and gently lift ①. If the door moves up and down, the screws in the hinges are loose. This happens to most hinges in heavy use (especially on exterior

doors). If the screws turn in the holes and keep on turning they have probably been tightened once too often and have lost their "bite" on the wood. In this case, back the screws out with a screwdriver or, if necessary, yank them out with pliers ②.

Then, either replace the screws with longer fatter ones (being careful that the heads will fully countersink in the hinge leaf) or plug the oversize holes with round toothpicks that have been covered with white glue. (By opening the door and wedging the corner you may be able to work on one hinge at a time, saving the trouble of removing the door.) When the toothpick plugs are thoroughly dry (several hours because of limited air circulation) trim the projecting ends of the toothpicks and drill new pilot holes for the original screws ③.

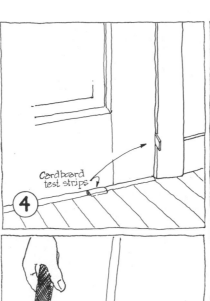

Cardboard test strips

④

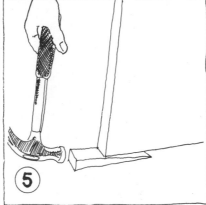

⑤

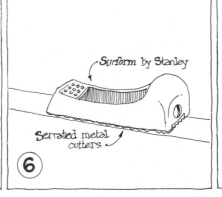

Surform by Stanley

Serrated metal cutters

⑥

If the door binds even after tightening the hinges, it will have to be planed. Find the exact location of the bind by sliding a thin cardboard along the crack. Mark the edges of the door where the card gets hung up ④. If the binds are on the top or the latch side of the door, there's no need to take the door off its hinges. Just open the door, put a wedge under the latch side, and go to work on it ⑤. A sharp **jack plane** is the ideal instrument here but a *Surform* tool ⑥ can also be effective. Even sandpaper wrapped around a block of wood will work if you're patient. And patient is what you should be, as too much cutting and not enough stopping to check the fit could result in a heat-robbing gap.

A door that binds on the hinge side or the bottom will have to

91

come off the hinges. First, mark the exact location of the binds and indicate the depth of the needed cut. As before, open the door part-way and slide a wedge under the corner on the latch side. Don't force the wedge in place — the purpose is to support the weight of the door without putting any thrust on the hinge pins. Next drive the hinge pins out with a screwdriver and light blows from a hammer 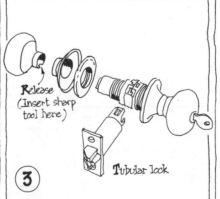. Remove the top pin last and be ready to support the door. Place the door on sawhorses or overturned chairs and use your plane, *Surform*, or sanding block to shave the offending edges.

Know your knobs. There are three kinds of knobs you're likely to run into (so to speak) in a rental. One is the older, mortise lock type ②. In this assembly the knobs are slid

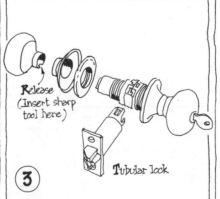

Mortise lock & knobs

②

Release
(Insert sharp tool here)

Tubular lock

③

onto a square shaft (**spindle**) and fastened with set screws. After loosening the screw and removing one knob, the spindle can be withdrawn by pulling on the other knob. Then take the **escutcheons** off by removing the screws ②.

Dwellings constructed after about 1950 will have **tubular locks**, an update of the mortise type. These became popular because the installation involved drilling rather than hand cutting a mortise. The escutcheon on this kind of knob is a "false front"— a decorative flange that must be pried from the flange underneath to get to the screws.

Knobs on tubular locks may have spring releases. You insert the tip of an icepick or a nail through a slot at the base of the knob, exert pressure and pull the knob away from the door ③.

Plugging the leaks.

If your place is like most uninsulated dwellings, almost half of the precious heat you put into it goes right out the windows and doors. All that, and mind you, the doors and windows are closed! The illustration ④ shows three types of insulation, all of which are likely to pay for themselves in a season of renting.

Adhesive-backed foam is the least expensive and easiest to install. It's also the shortest-lived; figure only a season of use. Before applying the adhesive foam, wash the door jambs thoroughly with grease-cutting detergent, then apply to the inside of the jamb, facing the door ④.

Wood strip with foam backing ④ is next in cost. It is nailed snugly against the outside of the closed door, top and sides. There it will be, like a sore thumb

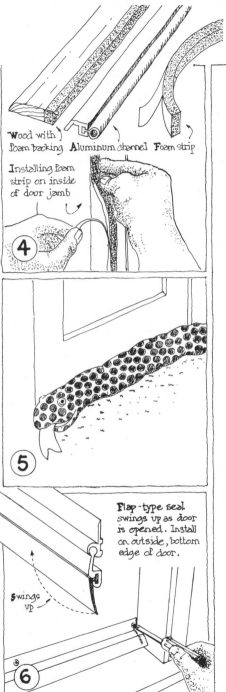

Wood with foam backing   Aluminum channel   Foam strip

Installing foam strip on inside of door jamb

④

⑤

Flap-type seal swings up as door is opened. Install on outside, bottom edge of door.

swings up

⑥

unless you stain or paint it to match the surround.

Aluminum channel with vinyl backing ④ is for when you're planning to stay several years and/or the owner pops for the materials. This stuff must be cut with a hacksaw and like the wood strip it gets nailed against the outside of the closed door.

To seal off drafts from the bottom of the door, you might want to buy or make a **door snake**— a long insulating pillow that is simply laid along the crack at the bottom of the door ⑤. It was good enough for Grandma. The main drawback is that it must be moved each time the door is opened. For more convenience, install an **aluminum and vinyl flap-type seal** on the outside bottom edge of the door ⑥.

Question one: Is there a door between your kitchen and living or dining area? Question two: Isn't it usually standing open? If so, there is reason to expect that a perfectly good, big, work table is just hanging there on its hinges, wasting away.

Fresh out of kitchen doors? Then check your abode for seldom-closed closet doors, or invest in a hollow-core door at your lumber retailer. Good prices are found on doors with cracks or holes in the plywood face, and one good side is all you need. Doors also show up occasionally in debris boxes.

Unhinge that door.

Assuming you've found a door that's still hanging, you can remedy that wasteful condition by removing the hinge pins: First, open the door part way and put a wedge under the side opposite the

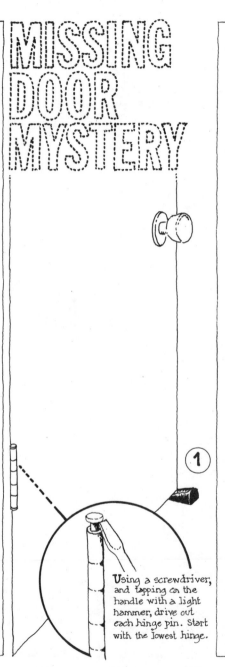

Using a screwdriver, and tapping on the handle with a light hammer, drive out each hinge pin. Start with the lowest hinge.

hinges. Easy does it — you only want to catch the weight of the door, not bind the hinges ①. Pull the top pin out while supporting the door with your other hand. Then, using the doorknob, pull the door straight away from the hinges. Now that it wants so much to be horizontal, you can begin to see its true potential as a table.

Remove the half hinges from the door and pin them back to their mates for safekeeping. If this looks tacky remove both halves and store screws, pins, and hinges in the box you designate for "house parts — to be reinstalled before moving." The exposed hinge pockets on the door casing may need to be painted.

Remove the door knob with help from p. 92.

If your door is of the modern, hollow-core type,

the face will be flat and ready for a wraparound cover. But if you have an older, panelled door, you'll need an additional surfacing material to span the pockets formed by the recessed panels. Use ⅛ inch untempered *Masonite* if your door has several small panels. Increase thickness to ¼ inch to span fewer, larger reveals.

Masonite by itself is an okay work surface, although dark and somewhat "cold" to the touch. It can be covered with the same materials I'll suggest for hollow-core doors – for example, the kind of sheet vinyl found in variety and fabric stores. Look for "tablecloth weight", not upholstery material – you'll know it by the gaudy patterns and colors. I use plain white, or if this is not available, some of the patterns are white on the reverse side. Buy enough to overlap your door by

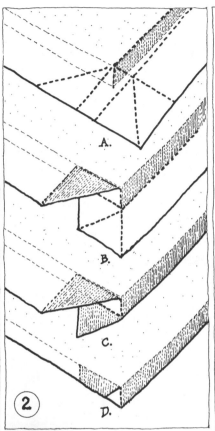

A.

B.

C.

D.

②

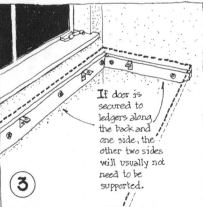

If door is secured to ledgers along the back and one side, the other two sides will usually not need to be supported.

③

6 to 10 inches on each side.

Lay the vinyl (good side down) on a clean rug or bare floor. Put the door (good surface down) on top of it. Adjust and trim so that there is an even 6 to 10 inches all around. Then begin wrapping and stapling, starting in the middle of the longer edges and working toward the corners. Fold and staple the ends last and to make neat corner folds follow the sequence in ②.

Next Question: What do you put your spiffy top on top of? Just about anything goes. Set it on two filing cabinets; sawhorses; a low chest of drawers; two cut-down cardboard barrels; or any combination of the above. If it's going into a corner the whole top can be supported with ledgers running along the back and one side ③. 🐌

DOOR STORAGE

I will bet there's at least one door in your place that is almost never closed. And chances are it's in the kitchen. Good. Behind that door is a great place to put all kinds of stuff.

① **Door Workshop.** Nothing helps get small jobs done like having the tools handy. The back of the kitchen door is about as handy as you can get. No kitchen door? This scheme will also work on the back of a cupboard door.

Canvas carpenter's apron can be hung on door with extra long push pins, or suspended from a brass grommet in each corner.

This is simply the basic tool kit, as described on p. 19.

② **Backpack Rack.** Two problems solved here: Where to store your backpack — (and backpacking stove, lantern, utensils, etc. — when you're not on the trail ...) and where to put awkward, infrequently used kitchen equipment like cookie sheets, muffin tins, colander, and such.

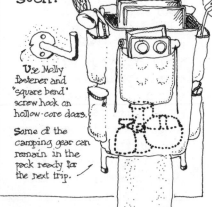

Use Molly fastener and "square bend" screw hook on hollow-core doors.

Some of the camping gear can remain in the pack ready for the next trip.

③ **Custodian's Closet.** Cut two 12" wide pine boards and screw them to the door. Attach metal clips: to the boards. Now you can arrange mop, broom, dust pan, and all that other cleaning paraphernalia on these boards. They move easily and set up quickly in your next place. A stapled-on plastic wastebasket will hold cleaners and other small items.

4 **Swing-out trays** can be mounted on the door or on the wall behind the door. They'll hold tools, sewing goods, office supplies, etc; ten high-impact polystyrene trays, dividers, and labels, about $13.00 from *The Horchow Collection* (and other mail-order houses).

Ten connected drawers swing from a single wall mount.

5 "Whatever happened to the coat closet?" "Well, you see... in this floor plan, the coat closet is the bathroom." "Then where do I hang my guests' wraps?" "Why, on the back of the door of course."

This easy-to-construct unit hangs on back of door with just two fasteners.

6 **Hanging racks** come in many sizes and materials, from plated metal bicycle baskets to vinyl clad kitchen organizers. All will contribute to increased door storage by holding magazines, potatoes, or canned goods. Check J.C. Penney and others.

7 **The Bathroom** is another place that's usually shy of storage. Here is a comprehensive solution. It holds shampoo, soap, and other back-up supplies while adding to the lineal footage of towel racks. In floor plans with the toilet near the door, this unit can also hold toilet paper and magazines.

Extra length of this dowel forms handle. Remove to replace paper.

Wood screw secures it when in position.

INFORMATIVE DOOR

Doors come between people and the places they're going. So they are natural places to get their attention. These pages are about saying things to people – through the medium of doors.

① Blackboard Door. Blackboard paint will convert any smooth surface into a chalkboard. If painting the door itself would make you unpopular, paint a sheet of ⅛" *Masonite* that's door-size (or smaller) and mount it with foam tape.

② Pinboard Door. Cut ½" insulation board to fit the door. (Recess about ½" top and sides to clear door stops.) Wrap the board with a solid color fabric and staple it to the back. Mount it on the door with finishing nails around the perimeter.

Use the door to display postcards, invitations, news clippings, cartoons, shopping lists, and a calendar. Use yarn to rope off one section for important family notices.

Cut hole for doorknob

③ Mail Call. In a multi-person household it's essential to have one place where mail is brought, and better, sorted. The pinboard door keeps it up off a table top and visible at a glance.

J.C.   T.R.S.   M.Y.

④ Seed Sorter.

Seed packets are decorative additions to a pin board door. They also stay organized and may help remind you of planting times. Pin your gloves there too, and add a hook or two for small garden tools.

⑤ Dresser Door.

Mirror tiles make a quick and easy back-of-door mirror. Four of them starting at head height is all it takes to see yourself in one piece.
A round mirror at the top adds a certain whimsy to the ensemble.

Foam tape

Rabbeted half round molding can be used to cover edge of glass.

⑥ Pocket Door. A

24 pocket shoe bag for about $10 adds bright vinyl color and sculptural interest to a door while also providing handy storage. You can roll magazines and stuff them in the pockets. You can also store art supplies, or even shoes.

⑦ Bill Collector.

Shoe bags also serve to file bills and receipts (like the cubby holes in a roll-top desk). Gummed labels can help code the pockets.

⑧ Carpet your doors

with self-stick carpet tiles and create a sound-absorbing fingerprint resisting door that you can also pin notes to. As an added bonus, the door becomes a better insulator.

4
Underfoot

Under my own foot right now is rice-straw matting. In some ways it's the ideal floor covering. Here in my studio/workshop it's laid over a (thrift store) rug pad, which is over concrete. Where the floor tends to dampness there is polyethylene film (4 mil thickness) under the pad.

I've also lived with rice-straw matting laid over ugly wall-to-wall carpeting in a one-room houseboat. Part of the room was a studio kitchen. As I think about it now, I wonder why I didn't lay plastic under the mats and over the carpeting there. But what with the boat gradually sinking (worms were eating away the Styrofoam flotation) I guess a few spills soaking through to the carpet were not my greatest worry.

Even here on the West Coast (close to the Asian source) I've seen the price of rice-straw go from 19 cents per square foot ten years ago to a current 50 to 80 cents. That makes it about $4.50 to $7.50 per square yard*, or close to the price of low grades of commercial carpeting.

Still, I think it approaches an ideal nomadic floor covering. First, it's modular. You can snip it apart along the edges of any squares, and restore sections by sewing in new squares. So it's easily adaptable to any floor plan.

It's also an excellent, neutral color that reflects a good amount of light, yet doesn't show dirt. That last quality is also one of its few drawbacks: Dirt (including rice-straw dust) sifts through the fibers and ends up on whatever's under it. Vacuuming

gets some, but not all of this. Plastic underlayment can help.

So *is* this the ideal floor covering? Well, I'd give it high marks if you're not prone to dust allergies.

But since it is short of perfect, and I promised not to make choices for you, turn the page for a bunch of alternatives.

*Rice straw seems to be a loosely applied generic term for woven natural rugs from several different materials. I've seen "woven sea grass" (coarse, and with a definite greenish cast), and also "maize" and "rush."

J. C. Penney's version is called "rice straw." Their 9 × 12 size is 55 cents per square foot.

Pier 1 Imports is another source; also *Cost Plus* (San Francisco Bay Area) and *Conran's* (you have to go to the stores; they have a country-wide mail order service for some items, but not this one).

101

Layovers

I've had enough experience with floor coverings to know that making recommendations is risky. Materials used to cover floors are subject to wear, spilled food, chemicals, and moisture conditions that are hard to predict. I've lived with a concrete floor that had to be repainted every year because of a mysterious problem with dampness. Later, I used the same paint on a wooden floor built right over a damp crawl-space and got great results. I like to see area rugs artfully arranged on a varnished wooden floor, but I've also been there when I had to pick startled guests off the floor after they've spun out on the same rugs.

So, here are the prices, again arranged in order of cost per square foot. My comments are here, too. But each situation is different. If you're thinking of spending some real money, I suggest buying a small sample of the material and trying it out in the planned location. Walk on it a while, try cleaning it, live with it a month, and you'll know if it's right.

COST/ SQ. FT.	MATERIAL	PRICE AS SOLD	COMMENTS
.03	FLOOR AND DECK PAINT (See p. 104)	@ 8.95 / gallon Covers 300 sq. ft.	Spend some time preparing the surface. Remove all wax and grease. Apply with roller. Let it dry!
.03	POLYETHYLENE FILM (4 mil. thickness)	@ 5.99 for a 10' x 20' roll	Use under porous floor coverings – rice-straw, ungrouted ceramic tile, wood tiles, etc.
.31	100% POLYESTER ROOM-SIZE RUG (foam backing)	@ 29.99 for a 8'-6" x 11'-6" rug	Can be machine-washed and dried in commercial-type machines. Good for edge-banding (p. 106)
.39	PLACE & PRESS VINYL FLOOR TILES	@ .39 / 12" sq. tile	Most patterns are fake something — the fake brick looks okay.
.39	100% POLYPROPYLENE OLEFIN CARPETING	@ 3.49 / sq. yard in 12' wide rolls	All-weather foam-backing. Can be used over concrete garage floors or over existing carpet.
.41 A*	KNOTTY PINE PANELLING BOARDS	@ 1.49 for each 1" x 6" x 8' length	Has shiplap vee-joint: ▨◣ Can be laid over existing floor by nailing to stringers.
.44	100% NYLON LEVEL-LOOP CARPETING	@ 4.99 / sq. yard (12 foot wide)	This is representative of several low-pile foam-backed nylon roll carpetings.

102   *A = Additional sealer required – adds to cost.

COST / SQ. FT.	MATERIAL	PRICE AS SOLD	COMMENTS
.48	POLYPROPYLENE CARPET SQUARES	@ .48 / 12" square (in cartons of 50)	Can be used in kitchen or bath. Individual squares can be replaced if damaged.
.55	RICE STRAW MATTING	@ 59.95 for a 9' x 12' section	See p. 101 for complete discussion.
.83	ARTIFICIAL GRASS "Astroturf"	@ 4.99 / linear foot foot 6' wide	Could be fun to use in a bathroom or kitchen; or line a shower with it.
.89	NYLON "ORIENTAL" CARPET (Machine printed)	@ 99.99 for a 9' x 12½' rug	Scotchguard for spill resistance. Does not look as much like the real thing as a wool version.
.89	FLOOR TILE VINYL (Self-adhesive — no wax)	@ .89 / 12" square	Can be put over existing linoleum or tile and removed with alcohol solvent.
.92	NYLON CARPET TILES (Self-adhesive — shag 5⁄8")	@ .92 / 12" square (in carton of 50)	Shag helps hide seams for a continuous carpet look. Individual squares can be replaced.
.99 to 1.99	MOSAIC CERAMIC TILE	@ .99 to 1.99 / 12" sheet-mounted on gauze	Can be laid over linoleum, vinyl tile, or concrete floors, and grouted with flexible bathtub caulk.
1.00 A	CORK SLABS (Dark brown — coarse)	@ 2.99 / 12" x 36" slab — 3⁄8" thick	Fragile until laid flat. Not possible to seal joints. Seal surface with varnish or plastic oil.
1.08 A	CORK TILES (Honey-colored — fine texture)	@ 9.75 for 9 tiles 2⁄10" thick (Conran's)	These are sold for walls or floors. Hold in place (for temporary installation) with double-face tape.
1.16	CEDAR CLOSET LINING (3⁄8")	@ 24.95 / package (covers 21.4 sq. ft.)	Intended for panelling, but thick enough for flooring. (Also tongue and groove.)
1.23	RED BRICK FACING	@ 6.77 / carton (covers 5-6 sq. ft.)	Meant for walls but can also look good on floors. Use vinyl bathtub caulk for flexible grout.
1.25	100% NYLON PLUSH (Jute backing)	@ 14.99 / running foot (12 feet wide)	Needs pad unless laid over existing carpet.
2.39	OAK FLOOR TILES Pre-finished / Foam cushion bk.	@ 2.39 / 12" square	On a fairly smooth, flat floor no adhesive is needed.
2.76	FLOKATI (100% wool)	@ 265.00 for an 8' x 12' rug (Penney's)	This may sound extravagant, but this popular fleecy white rug will hold its value. It's washable.
2.90	100% WOOL "BELGIAN" ORIENTAL CARPET	@ 279.00 for a 8'-3" x 11'-6" rug	These 100% wool rugs have the reproduction designs woven in. They need professional cleaning.

PAINT YOURSELF INTO A CORNER

I like that title — it's such a perfect picture of a self-made dilemma. These pages really are about painting yourself from corner to corner, but hopefully without embarrassing mistakes.

In fact, painting a floor is an operation that should be approached with singular caution and respect. For one thing, it's a big change, and not likely to go unnoticed by the powers that be. I have painted floors in these situations: 1) The linoleum was cracked and badly worn, and the landlord was unwilling to pay for new linoleum(or anything) to cover it. 2) In another case the floor was part of a basement area that was not used except for storage. (I was carving out some studio-workspace.)

Another reason to approach floor painting with caution: If it's not done right, you'll have 1) a sticky mess, or 2) a coating that wears out so quickly it soon looks worse than before you started.

Okay, then — how to do it right. There are four crucial steps, and the first three are preparation, preparation, and preparation. Really. You've got

HOW TO SELECT THE RIGHT PAINT FOR FLOORS	
PAINT TYPE	USES
LATEX "ENAMEL" FLOOR PAINT	Concrete, wood, linoleum, or vinyl tile. Easiest to apply, fast drying — least durable.
ALKYD ENAMEL FLOOR PAINT	Longer-lasting than latex but slower drying and messier clean-up.
EPOXY, POLYURETHANE, POLYESTER FLOOR PAINTS	For extra washability and for hard traffic areas. Test for compatibility on an inconspicuous part of vinyl or linoleum.
CLORINATED RUBBER PAINT	Especially formulated for concrete floors. Adheres well, even to new concrete.

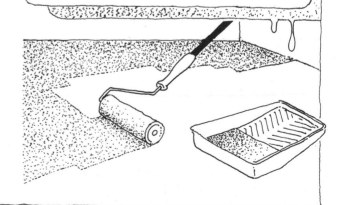

$32.⁰⁰/gallon

STRIPPER COAT

"Brush on STRIPPER COAT just as you would any paint. Allow 30 minutes to dry. Now you can paint your stage as often as you like with a water base paint and not harm the natural finish of the floor.

"When restoration is desired, merely strip the coating off. Floor will be left clean and unharmed. No kraft paper is needed for this product - STRIPPER COAT has a gray finish and from all appearances, looks and acts like a water base vinyl paint. It is also excellent for protecting props prior to any painting. Original finish can be restored easily after the show."

—Mutual Hardware Corp. Catalog
(Theatrical equipment and supplies.)

PAINT TRICK

To make your rooms seem bigger, at least visually, paint baseboard the same color as the floor. If your baseboards are narrow, or nonexistent, paint them in. (See also p. 55.)

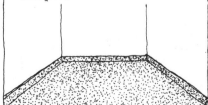

to be sure the floor will accept the paint. You remove all dirt, grease, and wax with a good detergent. (Or make your own — one cup household ammonia per gallon of hot water.) Then let it dry thoroughly — be sure even the cracks and seams are dry. Cracks in wood or linoleum floors can be filled with flexible bathtub caulk. Cracks in concrete can be filled with a product like *Porion*. (See p. 132.) Sand the filled areas if necessary, sweep or vacuum the dust, and go over the repaired area with a wet sponge mop.

When everything is dry again, you're ready to apply the paint. But not just any paint. Use only paint that's formulated for floors. The latex-base floor paints are good, and have the great advantage of drying fast enough to put the furniture back in 12 hours. Heavy tables or appliances should either wait outside an additional 12 hours, or should be shifted once or twice until the paint is dry clear through. Latex paints can be applied with a roller. After the lengthy preparations, painting is a delight. Gravity makes painting floors a snap.

Enamel floor paints are fumy, and slow-drying, (48 hours is not unlikely) but they are the most durable. From a health standpoint (the toxic solvents become airborne in both manufacture* and application) I recommend more frequent floor painting with latex than a single application of enamel. However, with a concrete floor subject to moisture from below, or in other difficult situations, enamel may be the best choice. Plan to paint Saturday A.M., then go away for the weekend.

Go to it, but remember your escape route. Don't paint yourself into a corner. ✒

* See note about oil-base paints on p. 27.

CARPETRY

Of all the investments you make in your moveable nest, carpeting may be the most costly. There are several ways that this expenditure can be justified: 1) Carpet is often a replacement for other expensive furnishings. A well padded carpet and a few big pillows may be all the furniture you need. 2) Floors are important. They're likely to be the surfaces that everybody who enters your place will notice. And 3), carpet is an excellent insulator, both from cold floors and from excessive noise. Nothing else you put in a room is likely to give you such a real and imagined feeling of "warmth."

Space Making.

Rugs are also an excellent means of making one room feel like two. A sea of wall-to-wall carpeting gains a secure island when you put a rug in the middle. Another rug in the corner announces that this is a quiet place to read or watch TV. Two tatami grass mats under a table define a dining area and also protect carpet from food spills ①.

Rugs on Rugs.

Foot traffic on a small rug usually causes it to migrate across the room. Staples or tacks will solve the problem but

they put lots of stress on one small part of the rug. *Velcro tabs* are a gentler alternative. You can get a *Velcro Rug Holder* kit complete with adhesive at hardware and housewares stores ②.

Edge Banding.

Carpet is a great cover-up. But if you need to cover a whole floor you're going to have to deal with the irregularities around the edges. Rather than cut expensive carpeting to fit this special case, consider running a two to three foot band of inexpensive carpeting (polypropylene or nylon)

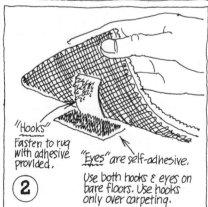

"Hooks" Fasten to rug with adhesive provided.

"Eyes" are self-adhesive. Use both hooks & eyes on bare floors. Use hooks only over carpeting.

around the edge. Then concentrate your investment on a good rug for the center of the room — one you can also use in your next place or even sell if you need to.

Overlapping the edge-band carpeting with the centered rug will give you added flexibility. In your next place you can reverse the edge that has been specially tailored and cut the other edge to fit around the new pattern of obstructions 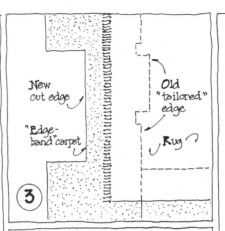. Any discrepancy in the height of the two pieces can be adjusted with the use of rug pads 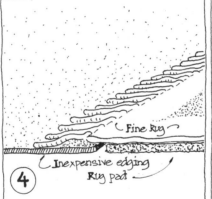.

Rolling Back the Rugs.

Once you discover there's a great hardwood floor under those dull green wall-to-wall carpets you'll be tempted to pull them up. Well, hold on a bit. Ripping them up is not so bad, but if you're doing it

New cut edge

"Edge-band" carpet

Old "tailored" edge

Rug

③

Fine Rug

Inexpensive edging Rug pad

④

Mat knife

⑤

with the idea of putting it back when you go, be aware of the pitfalls. First, you must roll the carpet around a cardboard tube or risk permanent crease and fold marks. Then think about where you're going to put this heavy monster. The pad needs to be rolled and stored too. And the tack strips pried up without breaking them.

One rather radical alternative is to cut a piece of the carpet away and expose a "dance floor" of bare wood 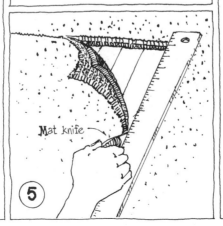. The carpet can be taped back in place and the cut line will be nearly invisible.

Another option is to pull up only the carpet. Leave the pad as a base for your own carpet or wall-to-wall grass mats. The finish level of the floorcovering remains about the same so you won't need to trim the bottoms of any doors. 🐌

A Bow to the East

It occurs to me that rice straw matting may work better in its country of origin. In Asia, the supremely civilized tradition of taking off your shoes before you enter the house means that floor coverings can be much more fragile — as well as light-colored and clean enough to sleep on. Suppose you made this a rule in your house — in the bedroom — or in the whole space. Provide a bench just inside the door; maybe some comfortable slippers; put up a sign as a gentle reminder for guests. Then notice how your floorcovering options have expanded.

Bedspread Rugs. The one shown here was my living room carpet. It went wall-to-wall in one corner, leaving a strip of bare wood floor along the main traffic path. The black and white design, rather than being overpowering, had a complementary, even a sharpening effect on any color placed near it. This one was an import from Spain, all wool, and cost about 45 dollars in 1970. It was a full size spread: 96 by 112 inches.

Quilted Mover's Pads, now coming into retail outlets as a high tech fashion item, have great possibilities as lightweight floorcoverings. A similar look, only in bigger sizes and at less cost, is available with channel-quilted bedspreads. *J.C. Penney*, for example, has 65% polyester, 35% cotton bedspreads in any of eight good rich colors, 120 by 118 inches for about fifty dollars. Remember, you can use it for many years (maybe someday even as a bedspread).

Cork is a comfortable, good looking floor covering. Without shoe traffic, you can use relatively inexpensive cork wall tiles on the floor. J.C. Penney has them for 42 cents each 12 by 12 inch tile (3/8 inch thick) provided you buy a package of 48. This is for the dark colored non-stick variety. You can put them down on any smooth wood, tile or linoleum floor using double-stick carpet tape. Lighter colors and self-adhesive tiles in the same size are 75 to 94 cents each. (These are harder to remove from most surfaces than carpet tape.) For greater durability, coat tiles with plastic-oil sealer.

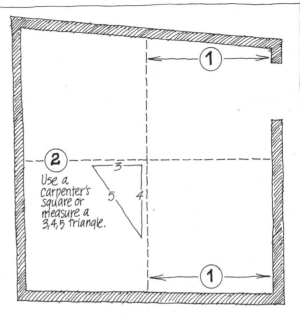

Use a carpenter's square or measure a 3,4,5 triangle.

Step-by-Step Tile Laying For the Fanatic

This floor plan of a room is exaggerated to make a point: the walls of most rooms are not exactly parallel to each other. Tiles will look okay, though, if

A) they are laid parallel to the wall from which you usually enter the room, and

B) the remnant tiles along the edges are not narrow slivers.

① Draw a line near the center of the room parallel to the wall with the entry.

② Establish a line perpendicular to line ① by the methods shown in the drawing above.

③ Trial fit a row of tiles in all four directions along these guide lines. Adjust so that the remnant tiles are half a square or more.

Tatami Mats. Sold in import stores as beach mats, these woven grass mats are the traditional Japanese floor coverings which also form the modular basis for Japanese architecture. Rooms are laid out in multiples of the approximately three by six foot mats. The size of the mats is, in turn, based on the space of one sleeping person. (Not one who thrashes a lot.) Mats can be stapled to most floors or they can be stitched along the edges and laid with double-stick carpet tape. They also can be used to cover walls.

109

5
The
Clean
Room

It was the bathroom (powder room? lavatory? WC?) in my present home that led me, maybe *drove* me, to put together this book. Most of the house looked just right for us, but the bathroom was something else.

There's a certain period in American history when the whole nation seems to have gone absolutely bonkers over weird color combinations. I remember the fads coming in waves—heliotrope and aqua was first; then black and purple; then pink and gray. It was an era—the late fifties—when you could order a Buick in *three* different colors.

The Buicks, thankfully, have been melted down. But the whimsy of the Eisenhower years is immortalized in my pink-and-gray ceramic-tile bathroom.

I knew I was up against a fairly permanent monument, but I vowed to somehow cover up, distract, or disguise this anomaly. The rest of the place was worth it.

Necessity is the mother of this chapter. But don't think the ideas came easy. 🐌

What do you do with pink tile?

1.

Deny it.

when present in equal intensities, they add up to white light. From this principle is derived this bathroom-lighting triad. With it, you can make a room any color you want it to be.

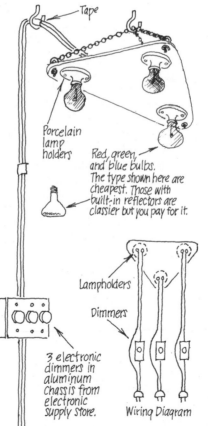

Tape

Porcelain lamp holders

Red, green, and blue bulbs. The type shown here are cheapest. Those with built-in reflectors are classier but you pay for it.

Lampholders

Dimmers

3 electronic dimmers in aluminum chassis from electronic supply store.

Wiring Diagram

2.

Re-light it.
You've seen foot lights on a theater stage haven't you? They're red, green, and blue for a reason. With color pigments you mix magenta, yellow, and turquoise blue to get all the other colors. But with lights, red, green, and blue are combined to yield all other colors and,

3.

TILE PAINT

Paint it.
Yes, there is a paint specially formulated for covering tile. It's permanent. It can be scrubbed, even with cleansers, and it wears well. I have seen it used on bathroom counter tops, even in ceramic sinks. I haven't yet had personal experience with it, but it appears to solve one of the big drawbacks of tile: the porous dirt-catching quality of the grouted cracks. You put this paint over tile <u>and</u> grout.

4.

Paint it out.

This was my solution. I brought home maybe 30 different paint chips from the paint store and looked at them next to the pink tile – in daylight and night light. When I thought I had one, I got a returnable (*Standard Brands Stores*) can of it and put just a swab next to the tile. I looked at it some more. Then I painted the whole room with it (except the tile and the ceiling). It was a rust red, and it effectively changed the color of the tile, from

baby pink to a dusty salmon. It also made the room insufferably dark, so I added an upper layer of a very compatible peach color.

5.

Cover it.

First, be sure the walls are thoroughly dry. Then cover them with black polyethylene film. Slit it into strips and fasten it at intervals with duct tape. (A 2 inch wide tape sold to seal heating ducts.) Now make panels of primed artist's canvas on 1" by 2" frames:

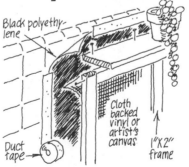

Black polyethylene
Cloth backed vinyl or artist's canvas
Duct tape
1"x2" frame

Or stretch and staple *tatami mats* (see p. 109) onto artist's stretcher bars:

(see p. 109)

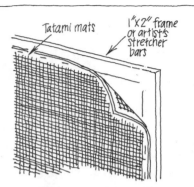

Tatami mats
1"x2" frame or artist's stretcher bars

Or make tambour-like rolls with redwood or cedar lath:

Black polyethylene
Lath

The black polyethylene acts as a moisture barrier and also keeps the wall from showing through.

6.

Well, maybe it's time to move.

Bath sheet suspended from the ceiling

THROW IN A TOWEL OR TWO

As wall-covering material, towels are on the expensive side: about 70 cents a square foot. But look at it this way: towels are already hemmed; they come in a range of colors; they are washable and durable; and they _feel_ good — especially in the bathroom.

(1) No problem justifying the expense here — these towels earn their keep. They form a colorful wainscoting until you need to dry your bod'; then they pop off for use as... get this... <u>towels</u>. Stretched onto the screws again, they are in a good place to dry quickly.

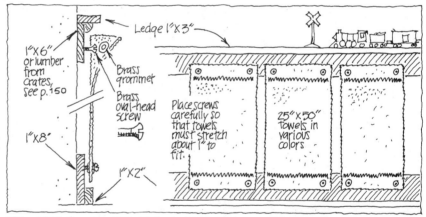

Ledge 1"x 3"

1"x 6" or lumber from crates, see p.150

Brass grommet

Brass oval-head screw

1"x 8"

1"x 2"

Place screws carefully so that towels must stretch about 1" to fit.

25"x 50" towels in various colors

(2) Towels look great with light coming through them. And they are also effective at stopping the view. Hung as shown here, they adapt to just about any size window and offer a modicum of insulating value.

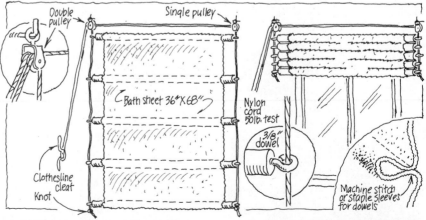

Double pulley

Single pulley

Clothesline cleat

Knot

Bath sheet 36"x 68"

Nylon cord 50 lb. test

3/8" dowel

Machine stitch or staple sleeves for dowels

(3) I saw the original of this overhead clothes dryer in Hal and Linda Bennett's house. They ran it along the hallway which gave it extra length and maybe drier air than you would get if you put it in a bathroom. It would also work on a backporch or balcony.

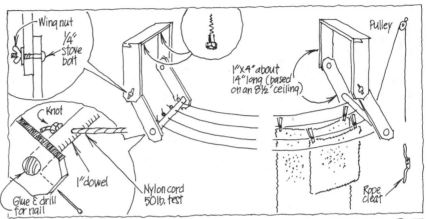

(4) Panels of 1/8 inch pegboard are an inexpensive way for you to bring your own walls into a bathroom. Use them to cover wallpaper you can't remove. Painted with semi-gloss latex they are water-resistant. Water vapor will go through the holes, though, so a polyethylene vapor barrier is a good idea. (See p.113)

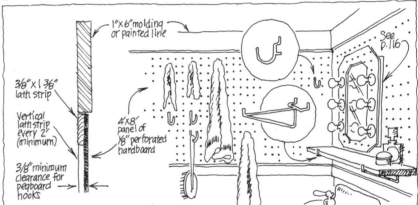

(5) This towel-hanging panel of poultry netting can be varied in proportion from a chair-rail-height panel to a wall-covering series of panels. The net itself is transparent, but will screen the wall somewhat if painted white. (See p.125)

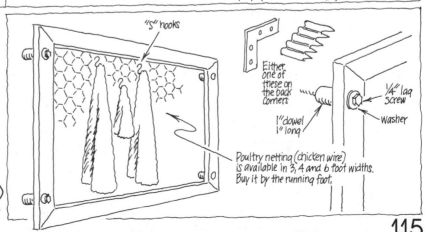

Bath Basics

I'square double-sided foam tape designed for humid application

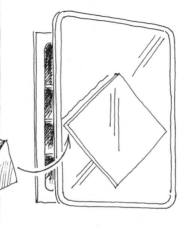

I was having trouble facing my reflection in the mornings. Then I noticed that it wasn't my face that was distorted; it was the cheap mirror on my medicine cabinet.

My first idea was to get a single 69 cent mirror tile and stick it (with foam tape) to the part of the medicine cabinet mirror where my face was staring back at me.

Another quick improvement was to make a frame of picture molding and fasten it, again using foam tape, to the sides of the mirror. This did nothing for my reflection but it did improve my spirits.

Picture frame molding or found picture frame

With a little more time and money it's possible to cover the original door with a new mirror, and then to add this pegboard frame, complete with make-up table lighting in the theatrical mold. If you alternate red, green, and blue lights in this setup and connect each color to a separate dimmer (see details, p.112) you have a mirror and lighting that could make Walter Matthau look 25.

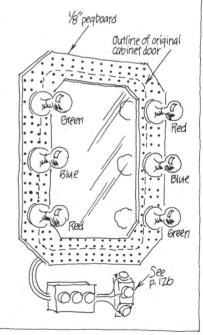

1/8" pegboard

Outline of original cabinet door

Green

Red

Blue

Blue

Red

Green

See p.126

While we're at it, here are a few other basic improvements that could make your bathroom more livable.

For storage of clean towels, soaps, and other bath supplies how about a top file and drawer unit? They're about 50 dollars brand new, but you can pick one up for half that at a used office furniture store. One spray can of white enamel or a bright primary color will bring it out of the office world.

towels and toilet paper

shampoo, soap, etc.

multi-colored labels

While making the rounds of used furniture stores, keep an eye peeled for sections of gym lockers. These are great for bathrobes, towels, and small items storage. Since they sport louvered ventilation you can even put wet towels in here:

For towels and clothes that are past reusing there is the open laundry sorter. It has a bin each for colors, whites, and special-treatment washables. Dimensions are 33 by 14 7/8 by 28 inches high.

Open laundry sorter has denim-look liner. Folds for storage #17.99 @ Sears.

And then there is this cheap and easy towel holder.

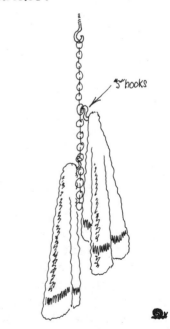

5" hooks

SHOWER POWER

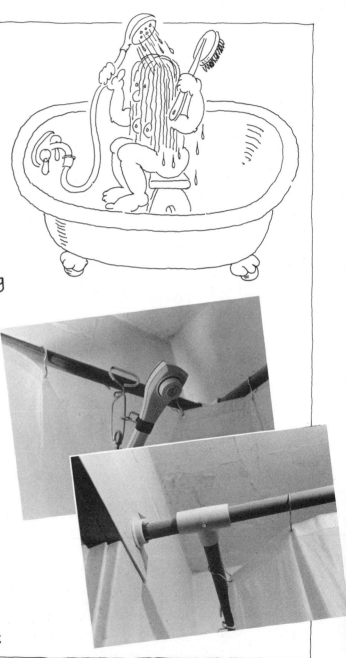

There are a couple of conditions I put at the top of my list when looking for a new rental: To be in the running at all, the place has to have a gas stove. Second in importance is a shower — not just a tub. Replacing an electric stove is not something I'd consider, but if a place were to my liking in most other ways, I <u>would</u> — and have — rigged my own shower. Here are several ways I've found to start from scratch, or improve an existing shower.

(1) First of all, it's good to remember that most of the world and our recent ancestors got along quite well without showers. In most of Greece, according to my friend Stephen Spano, most everybody sits on a low stool in a tub and uses a hose to shower. Since simple solutions are often the best (and this is one I lived with for a year or more) I'll give a respectful nod to the three-dollar rubber shower hose. You can even get one at the all-night grocery.

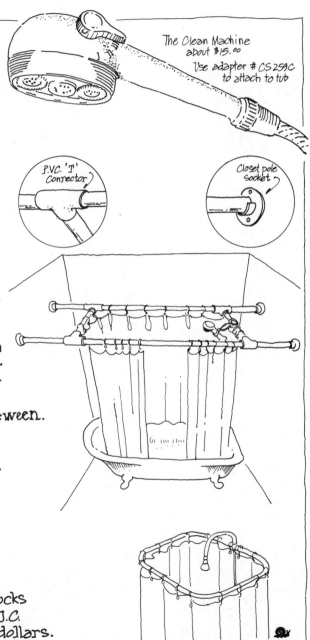

The Clean Machine
about $15.00

Use adapter # CS259C
to attach to tub

P.V.C. 'T'
Connector

Closet pole
socket

(2) The next step up is an add-on shower attachment, sometimes called a telephone shower ~ basically it's a rubber shower hose with pretensions. The best ones, like the *Clean Machine* (*Chicago Specialty Mfg. Co.*) have adjustments to give several different spray patterns from full spray to pulsating pleasures. Now if you're going in for the wild stuff you'll definitely need a wrap-around shower curtain.

(3) For a quick and economical shower and curtain addition to a tub, Bill Well's solution is the best I've seen. You need walls on three sides of the tub to support it, but that's fairly standard. You'll also need to buy enough closet pole (that's what your lumber merchant calls 1½"inch dowels) to run wall-to-wall at front and back of the tub, plus enough for two pieces to run in between. Also pick up four closet pole sockets, and four T connectors in 2 inch diameter PVC (plumbing department).

Bill has a clever detail for holding the telephone shower head. He just cannibalized a metal clamp light. The base of the shower head takes the place of the light socket.

(4) If you'd rather spend a few more bucks and a little less construction time, J.C. Penney has a portable shower kit for 27 dollars.

6
The Cook Room

Okay, I've told you the bathroom in my place was a challenge. Well, you should have seen the kitchen. If pink and gray are the perfect colors for the fifties, then avocado-green must one day be the collectors' rage when the sixties become nostalgic. (Maybe quiet, dull avocado-green was the only possible response to eye-popping psychedelia.)

And yes, I do have avocado-green appliances. What follows, then, is the true story of a drab suburban kitchen and how it found new life.

APPLIANCE APPEARANCE

Maybe it's good that I can do my kitchen routine on automatic pilot. If I had to be at full attention, I'd miss out on a lot of daydreaming time. It's unfortunate, though, if I'm adapting to a routine that's full of needless extra operations. A little reorganization could save precious minutes, and with that extra time I could do some serious, undistracted daydreaming.

A whole wave of such step-saving changes followed the recent rehanging of my refrigerator door. (Not all refrigerators permit this, but it's worth checking out.) With the fridge finally opening toward the rest of the kitchen, some other needed changes became obvious. For one thing, I came out of the refrigerator, arms loaded, pointing in the right direction, but with nowhere to put things. Here was also my chance to provide a counter and also fix the stove in its ambiguous relationship to the refrigerator and the nearest counter.

The result is the stove has sprouted wings; the wall behind the stove has acquired lunch counter-like mirrors and shelves; and the back panel of the stove sports Mexican tile. I don't expect you'll have exactly the same kind of situations, but there are several ideas here,

Before

After

and maybe one will fit, or at least push a button for you. Here's how it was done.

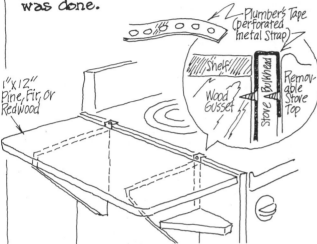

1"x12" Pine, Fir, or Redwood

Plumber's Tape (perforated metal Strap)

Shelf

Wood Gusset

Stove Bulkhead

Removable Stove Top

The wooden wings provide an insulated surface for things going on or off the stove. The method of attachment requires only four screw holes which are hidden from view.

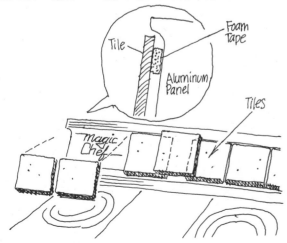

Foam Tape

Tile

Aluminum Panel

Tiles

Magic Chef

The tiles are a simple covering for an ugly aluminum backpanel containing nothing but the manufacturer's name and some photo-engraved wood panelling.

The mirrored back wall is 12 inch square mirror tiles fastened with double-faced foam tape.

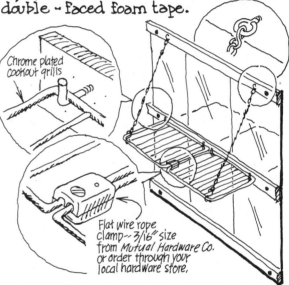

Chrome plated cookout grills

Flat wire rope clamp—3/16" size from *Mutual Hardware Co.* or order through your local hardware store.

For the finishing touch, the flaking chrome-plated plastic stove knobs were jettisoned in favor of standard replacement knobs from the hardware store.

Total expenditures: two weekends and about 15 dollars. The stove has turned the corner, functionally and aesthetically. My routine time in the kitchen is a bit more pleasant, my daydreams more sanguine. ✒

MORE COUNTER SPACE

The smallest kitchen I've ever cooked in was on the landing of a third floor attic apartment. The dish drainer rested on a hinged platform that dropped down in front of the bathroom door. This provided a very strong incentive to promptly dry and put away the dishes. Since those student days, I've cooked in the galley of a one-room houseboat, a studio apartment, and now I luxuriate in a kitchen that's 10 by 12 feet. Funny — in not one of them, including the present one, has there ever been enough counter space.

1 Stacks of wet dishes are terrible space grabbers. But I dislike drying and putting them away at least as much as you do. I've seen suggestions for dishracks built into cabinets. The cabinet has no bottom so the dishes can be put away, wet. The drips fall into the sink. That sounds fine, but I've never lived in a place with a cabinet over the sink. The variation shown here frees up the counters, lets the dishes drip into the sink, all without sacrificing the view. Add another shelf for plants.

2 This is a deceptively simple product. Just buy one (about five dollars) and you'll wonder how you ever got along without it. I got mine at a do it yourself lumber-hardware store.

Square bend screw hook

Wire letter trays & stacking posts from an office supply store.

Wood screw into dowel

Clamp (see p. 123)

Plate drying rack is really a file organizer (office supply)

1" dowel

Washer

Lag screw

Screw eye

Over-the-sink cutting board

3 These pine racks are popping up every-where. You can pay more, but the Asian imports work fine and cost only about four dollars. Put several against the back splash between counter and cupboards for added storage.

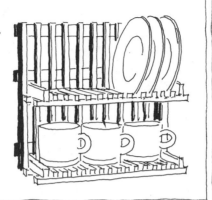

5 Hanging grids are great for vacant walls or even backs of doors. You can do the dowel grid (also shown on p. 43) or run some changes on the basic idea using poultry netting or chrome-plated cookout grills.

4 Save some drawer space by support-ing your silverware in this nifty organizer. Hang it on the outside of a cupboard or drawer, or on the wall next to your dining table. Buy this one from *L.L.Bean*, or make your own with wood salvaged from fruit crates.

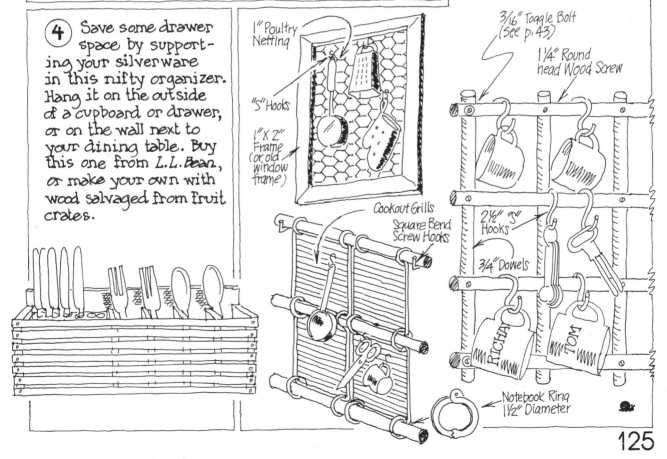

1" Poultry Netting

"S" Hooks

1"x 2" Frame (or old window frame)

3/16" Toggle Bolt (see p. 43)

1 1/4" Round head Wood Screw

Cookout Grills

Square Bend Screw Hooks

2 1/2" "S" Hooks

3/4" Dowels

Notebook Ring 1 1/2" Diameter

"4 in 1 Perma Plug" Quickly and neatly turns duplex outlets into fourplex.

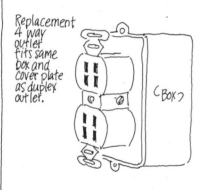

Replacement 4 way outlet fits same box and cover plate as duplex outlet.

(BOX)

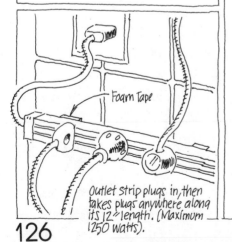

Foam Tape

Outlet strip plugs in, then takes plugs anywhere along its 12" length. (Maximum 1250 watts).

126

MORE POWER TO YOU

Good old buildings, the kind I prefer to live in, usually have bad old wiring. This comes to a head, most dramatically, in the kitchen. Now, I'm not a fan of electric can openers and electric bag closers, but I _do_ like to plug in my blender and coffee grinder without draping extension cords across the counter. Here are some ways I've found to bring the power where I need it.

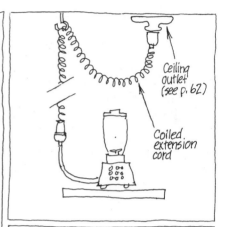

Ceiling outlet (see p. 62.)

(see p. 62.)

Coiled extension cord

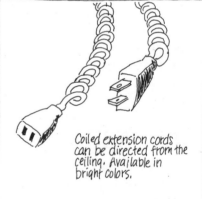

Coiled extension cords can be directed from the ceiling. Available in bright colors.

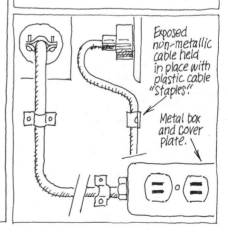

Exposed non-metallic cable held in place with plastic cable "staples."

Metal box and cover plate.

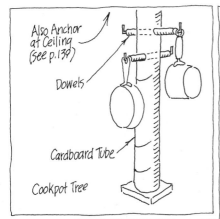

Also Anchor at Ceiling (see p.139)

Dowels

Cardboard Tube

Cookpot Tree

Screw Eye "S" Hook

Hard Rock Maple "Decor Deck" by Carborundum Co. (or build your own)

Screw Eye

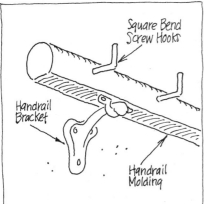

Square Bend Screw Hooks

Handrail Bracket

Handrail Molding

COOKPOTS AS ART OBJECTS

Several problems solved here, all having to do with the awkwardness of cooking utensils, pots and pans division. Here's my list of complaints: they're heavy; they take up valuable shelf space; they are a drag to wash and worse to dry. The pan you want is always on the bottom of the stack — the lid that fits is somewhere else entirely. Well here are six ways to turn that liability into something of an asset. Think of your kitchen as a workshop. Get yourself some good tools and put them out where you need them. You'll still have to wash them, but you can hang them up to dry. 🐌

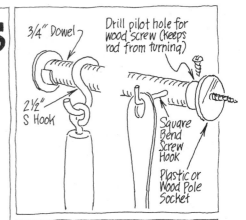

3/4" Dowel

Drill pilot hole for wood screw (keeps rod from turning)

2 1/2" S Hook

Square Bend Screw Hook

Plastic or Wood Pole Socket

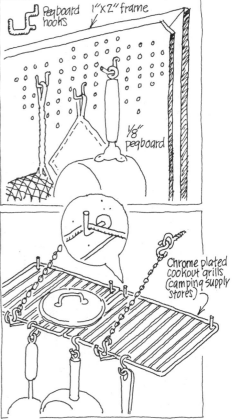

Pegboard hooks

1"x2" frame

1/8" pegboard

Chrome plated cookout grills (camping supply stores)

127

An Island in the Stream

Too much floor space – too little counter space. That's the common failing of kitchens built before the 1950's. Take mine, for example. (Please!) It's as if the designer (I hesitate over that choice of terms) took an old fashioned country kitchen plan and then lined two walls with modern cabinets and appliances. The rest of the space, which might, in older days, have held a big dining table – or a doughbin table – is just sitting there.

Sooo... what we have here is the updated version of the doughbin table: An island; a place to roll out dough, or put together a salad, or pour a drink, or grab a breakfast. It's based (literally) on a standard size ready-made kitchen cabinet. Depending on the material and finish, you can have a new one for 25 to 60 dollars, a used one for half that. Adding a nice wood top, hinges etc. puts on 15 to 30 dollars more.

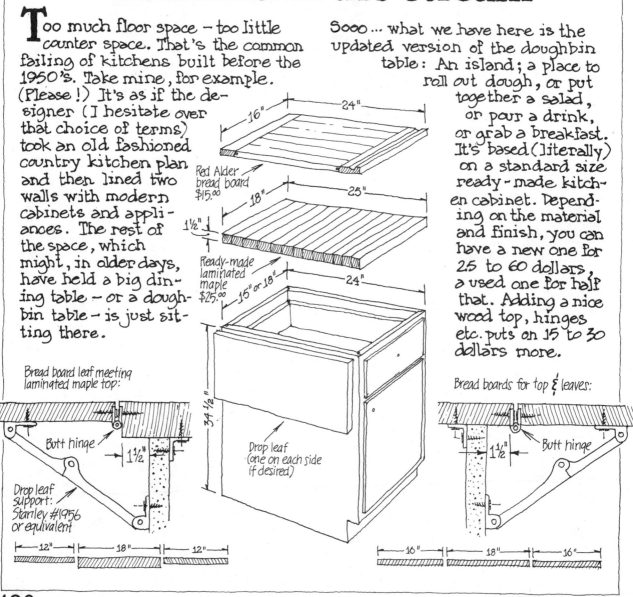

16"   24"

Red Alder bread board $15.00

18"   25"

1½"

Ready-made laminated maple $25.00   15" or 18"   24"

34½"

Drop leaf (one on each side if desired)

Bread board leaf meeting laminated maple top:

Butt hinge

1½"

Drop leaf support: Stanley #1956 or equivalent

12"   18"   12"

Bread boards for top & leaves:

Butt hinge

1½"

16"   18"   16"

Other "islands":

Less Expensive Island

3 tier utility table about $15.00 new, or get a used one and paint bright colors.

Laminated top, hardwood or fir, or bread board

Drill through handle and into top. Insert lag screws.

Rolling Breakfast Island

Cast metal base is salvaged from a treadle sewing machine. Other possible bases: old washtubs, tool stand, tree trunk (see also p. 132 & 133).

Laminated hardwood top or side of used cable spool

Rolling Island

Same as previous page but four-wheel drive model.

Towel rack and handle

Stationary Island

Fits next to a stove or at end of counter.

Maple, laminated fir, or bread-board top.

Plastic milk cartons (surplus stores).

Ball bearing swivel casters (with brakes) on one end; non-swiveling casters on other end.

7
Kidspace

Careful, now, this is touchy. Too much has already been published about top-down interior design for kids. Ever notice how those chrome and Formica rooms with their carefully made beds and artfully posed teddy bears never have any real children in them?

I think designers, for the most part, have approached children as if they were a native population ripe for religious conversion. Not enough has been allowed for kids' own budding architectural sense.

Snow forts, caves, tree houses, floating logs, deserted buildings, houses under construction—when I think about it, my childhood was full of spatial experiences. I can't remember how many holes (they must have been at least five feet deep) we dug in our sandy backyard in Michigan.

Think about it. Kids love extremes: dark, enclosed, tiny spaces for the drama of hiding; high platforms and climbing trees for the thrill of being above it all.

Sure, we've lost a lot of these opportunities by jamming ourselves closer together. All the more reason to be sure that kids' controllable inside spaces have something to do with their real needs.

FUNKY FURNITURE

These pages pay homage to Garth Williams's wonderful illustrations for <u>Goldilocks and the Three Bears</u>. As far as I can remember, that was my first encounter with the house-in-a-hollow-tree aesthetic and all that it implies: rustic bentwood chairs, peeled-log tables, and giant hearths made from rounded fieldstones. I am still hooked, and so, I suspect, are kids in the computer age. Forget High Tech...let's see more kids' rooms in Troglodyte Gothic! (Cheaper, too.)

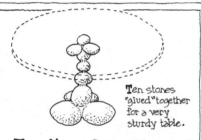

Ten stones "glued" together for a very sturdy table.

Furniture from Stones?
I admit, it may sound perverse. Yet a case can be made for stone as a logical building material, even for nomads like us. Example: You move to your new home. Quickly you locate a "quarry"— a not-too-distant stream or river. You borrow enough water-sculpted rocks to construct your project. When it's time to move again you break up your furniture and return the stones to their natural environment.

Besides stones, you'll also need some stone "glue"— also known as *Porion*. This is an adhesive filler containing quartz crystals in a synthetic resin. It's a non-toxic, workable, clay-like substance that dries as hard as stone.

Make a smooth fillet of *Porion* between stones.

Living With Trees.
Here is a drawing of a storage tree which spent some time in my son's room. I would have had a photo here, but before I could get to that the tree began to release piles of sawdust. Not

wanting to risk wood-boring beetles roaming about the house, we decided the tree should go back to nature for a time.

This makes a point about the romance vs. the reality of trees as furniture: Only truly dead trees make acceptable furniture.

Now don't get the idea you have to move to the country to find raw materials for these projects. Urban cast-offs can be just as inspiring. I made a neat bookshelf once from a discarded road barrier. Its black and yellow diagonal safety stripes had weathered to a soft abstraction. As this was to become a shelf for a telephone and related stuff I measured the biggest items (phone-directories) and cut two uprights a bit bigger. Then I divided the remainder of the board to get a top and bottom.

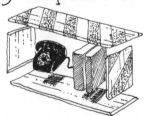

Working within such confines — there is this much material and no more — and at the same time restoring a throw-away to a new use — it's very satisfying work.

Some fine stools/storage cubes can be made from crate lumber. Look under "Motorcycle Dealers - New" in the Yellow Pages to locate sources. of crates. Also look for discarded or broken pallets wherever merchandise is unloaded with forklift trucks. Ask your kids. They probably pass such places on their path to and from school.

See also p. 150

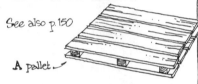

A pallet

Assemble the cubes with boards of varying widths. This gives an interlocking structure that requires no added bracing.

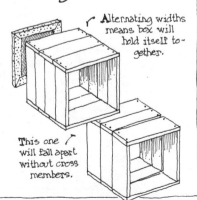

Alternating widths means box will hold itself together.

This one will fall apart without cross members.

A sturdy base for tables and benches can be made from a **concrete pier**. They're about a dollar apiece at builder's supply stores.

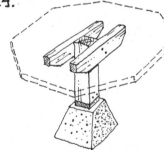

The wooden block that's cast into the top of the pier provides a means of attachment. A 4"x4" post can be toe-nailed into it. Supports for the table or bench top are attached to the 4x4.

None of these projects require expert carpentry nor fancy tools. No elaborate sanding and finishing. This is Saturday afternoon stuff ... everybody can help.

Kids love to get up in the world. Build one of these tower beds and kiss 'em good night without bending over.

This ① is similar to a loft bed I built in my first San Francisco apartment. Three lag screws were put into studs in the wall; the landlady saw it and didn't faint. This plan allows for several variations: the supports can be cardboard tubes, fence posts, or 4" by 4" posts.

A big project can be less awesome if you start with something that already exists. This bunk bed builds upon two sturdy steel shelving units as sold by Sears and many other outlets. Be sure to look for diagonal bracing on three sides, heavy-gauge steel posts, and ribbed shelves. Note the non-standard

TOWER BEDS

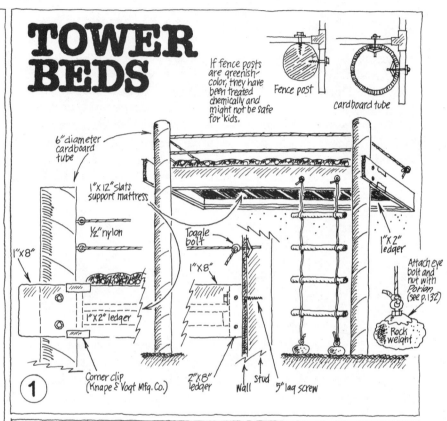

If fence posts are greenish-color, they have been treated chemically and might not be safe for kids.

Fence post

cardboard tube

6" diameter cardboard tube

1"x12" slats support mattress

½" nylon

1"x8"

Toggle bolt

1"x8"

1"x2" ledger

Attach eye bolt and nut with Forton (see p.132)

Rock weight

Corner clip (Knape & Vogt Mfg. Co.)

2"x8" ledger

Wall

Stud

5" lag screw

1"x2" ledger

①

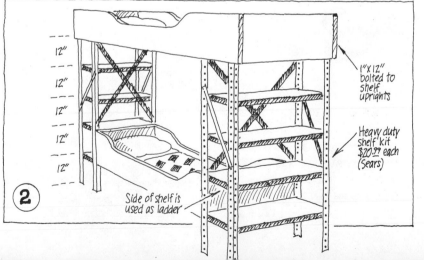

12"

12"

12"

12"

12"

1"x12" bolted to shelf uprights

Heavy duty shelf kit $20.99 each (Sears)

Side of shelf is used as ladder

②

shelf - spacing called
for in the drawing ②.

More tubes ③ —
this one is self - sup-
porting. The tent struc-
ture could be a fun ad-
dition to any of the
beds on these pages.
It uses patented plas-
tic brackets made by
Big A. The manufacturer
recommends taking a
bracket with you when
you're selecting 1" by 2"
struts because even
milled lumber can vary
enough to be a poor fit.

There's no specific
plan here ④; the idea
is to go with what you
have — or can find. By
collecting used chests
of drawers and build-
ing companion shelv-
ing units you can create
a self - contained island.
Think of it as a room
within a room: adapta-
ble to a shared room,
or to a teenager's need
to run the stereo up without driving the rest of
the household crazy.

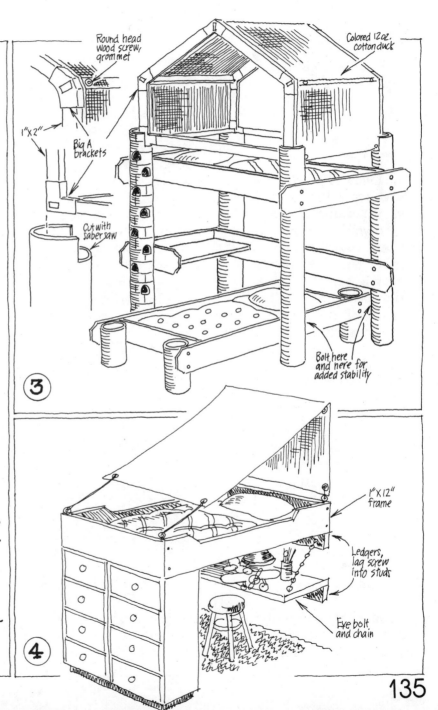

Round head
wood screw,
grommet

Colored 12 oz.
cotton duck

1"x 2"

Big A
brackets

Cut with
saber saw

Bolt here
and here for
added stability

③

1"X 12"
frame

Ledgers,
lag screw
into studs

Eye bolt
and chain

④

CURTAINS FOR YOU, KID

Humans must have some kind of inborn, very primitive fascination with hiding, we seem to do it so much. From infants who howl over a simple game like peek-a-boo, through years of hide-and-seek, to the adult equivalent—sailing away to a desert island (or simply pulling the covers over our heads).

Maybe because kids seem to be forever invading our privacy, we tend to invade or ignore theirs. But kids need privacy, too. Here are some ways to provide some friendly barriers with kids involved in the making.

A small investment in clay pots and saucers, potting soil, some string, and bean seeds, is all kids need to grow their own curtains. Kentucky Wonder, Scarlet Runner, and lima bean seeds will produce foliage even in a north-facing window, but you'll need daily sun for the flowering varieties. Allow about two to three weeks for coverage at cafe curtain level, a few weeks more for "full-length drapes."

Even very little kids can get involved in folding and dip-dyeing their own curtains. Do test folding and dye-ing with towel paper and food colors. When you get a design you all like, repeat it using cotton muslin and a permanent coloring like *Inkodye*, available at art stores. Get the information sheets that come with the dyes and follow directions carefully.

Inkodye resist is a clear paste that can be applied to any area where you don't want color or where you want to put a subsequent color. Resist can be applied with a brush but you'll have more drawing control if you put it in an applicator, like a mustard squeeze-bottle.

Again, do some experimenting with towel paper or scrap fabric. Many effects are possible. After the color is applied, the resist can be removed with hot water.

Once your fabric is dipped, drawn on, and dyed, you can hem it with fabric glue, iron-on basting strip, or by machine sewing. Hem a sleeve in the top and

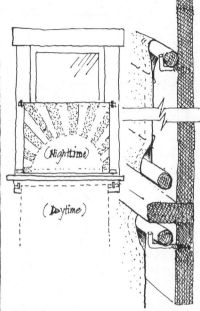

(Nighttime)

(Daytime)

bottom (use a small stapler or sew) and slide in a ½ inch dowel or length of ½ inch copper tubing. Measure and place four square-bend screw hooks as shown. At nighttime hang the curtain/banner from the top hooks. To open the drapes, simply rehang on the bottom hooks.

Curtains aren't limited to windows. They're also useful for dividing other parts of the room.

Here's a scheme for a sound cube using a frame made with *Big A* brackets and 1 by 2 inch lumber. It can be draped with colored canvas for visual privacy. For visual and auditory isolation, staple on one-inch foam, or carpet padding, or egg cartons glued to insulation board.

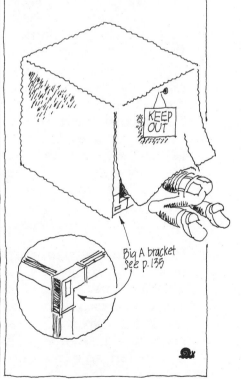

KEEP OUT

Big A bracket
see p. 135

137

TUBATECTURE

That means architecture made from tubes. Where do you get tubes? Two ways: 1) Call or nose around shops that sell floor coverings. Both linoleum and carpets come rolled on sturdy cardboard tubes. They range in size from 2 inches (diameter) to 6 or 8 inches. You can usually have them free for the asking. ('Tell them you're doing projects with kids.) Or, you can pick them out of the debris box after closing time. Also visit fabric stores and upholstery shops. They'll have the smaller diameters. The second approach is to buy tubes from a company that sells them as forms for pouring concrete columns. These cardboard tubes are super-sturdy, and go from 8 inches up to 20 inches (inside diameters). You'll find sources listed under "concrete forms" or "concrete products" in the Yellow Pages. A brand name to look for is *Sonotubes*.

Basic Tubesmanship. Tubes can be cut and drilled with ordinary woodworking tools. The same fasteners will work, as will the same glues used for wood. Tubes can be painted, but a first-coat of shellac may be needed as a sealer. Or use the recommended primer for the paint you intend to use. Latex-base paint works best. A fast and neat way to decorate the tubes is with self-adhesive papers like *Contact*. Try the silver and gold foil for space ships, and the brick pattern for old forts. By all means invite the kids' ideas at the earliest planning/purchasing stages.

You can also use ordinary aluminum foil wrapped and fastened with double-faced tape. Any kind of fabric or cloth-backed vinyl can be wrapped around the tubes using staples or a paste made from equal parts of white glue (*like Elmer's*) and water.

Start Here. This first project will give you some fast, gratifying results and a chance to ease into tube carpentry. Cut a 6 to 8 inch carpet or linoleum tube into 20 inch lengths. Glue the tubes together to make a base for a table. Use the same idea to make stools.

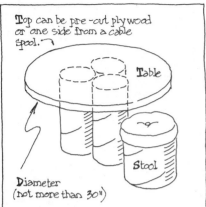

Top can be pre-cut plywood or one side from a cable spool.

Table

Stool

Diameter (not more than 30")

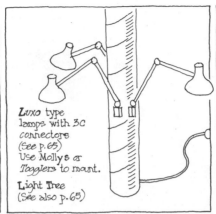

Luxo type lamps with 3C connectors (See p. 65) Use Mollys or *Togglers* to mount.

Light Tree (See also p.65)

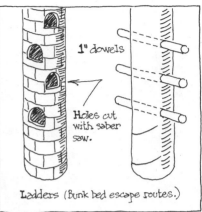

1" dowels

Holes cut with saber saw.

Ladders (Bunk bed escape routes.)

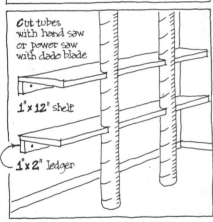

Cut tubes with hand saw or power saw with dado blade

1" x 12" shelf

1" x 2" ledger

Adjustable Pole Jack
Locks tubes in position by pressure against ceiling:

Use with Light Tree Ladders and Shelves.

Hex-head machine screw

Wood block

'T'-nut

Glue & nail

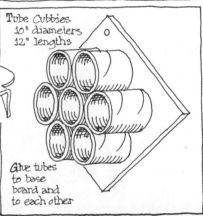

Tube Cubbies
10" diameters
12" lengths

Glue tubes to base board and to each other

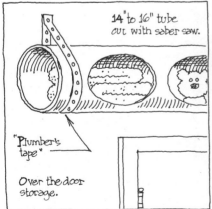

14" to 16" tube cut with saber saw.

"Plumber's tape"

Over the door storage.

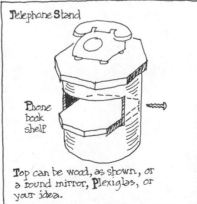

Telephone Stand

Phone book shelf

Top can be wood, as shown, or a round mirror, Plexiglas, or your idea.

8
Stowage

A good storage system is right at the core of the successful moveable nest. It's what keeps your growing collection from becoming a burden. It's also the bag of tricks from which come the changes that keep your nest lively and interesting.

Good storage may also be crucial to your carrying out the fine print of your rental agreement. If you remove parts of your rental property—as I encourage you to—you are obligated to put them back. Not doing this might even cost you your rental deposit. You *can* get it all back together and feel freer to take it apart if you label and store all dismantled parts in a systematic way.

Good storage also makes moving much more bearable. It means that items you haven't used since your last move are still in their labeled boxes. If you still can't bear to throw them out, at least you don't have to pack them again.

This chapter is also about seeing the necessity of moving as an opportunity. Your accumulated possessions are parts and pieces of your personal history. Moving gives you the impetus to review this material just as you might occasionally review the entries in a journal. To push the analogy a little further, good storage is to your collection of belongings as neat handwriting and careful dating are to a good journal. 🐌

Better Boxes

Buckminster Fuller, the poet/engineer/futurist and frequent mover has observed that people moving out of apartments carry away mostly the same items the new tenants will soon be bringing in. If you've ever stayed in a furnished house you'll probably agree: Most people's living tools are pretty much alike and can be quite comfortably interchanged, at least for a time. But the need to have at least some of their own things around them is strong for most people, and for frequent movers it may be a matter of survival.

(1) **I support the habit;** I know that some personal things are worth their extra weight in security alone. They help make you feel whole when your life is full of variables. I'll just suggest that the effect is enhanced and the habit kept in bounds by knowing exactly what you <u>are</u> carting around.

To this end here are several ways to organize your baggage, before or after (preferably not <u>during</u>) your next move:

I just recently became aware of the terrific boxes sold by U.S. Post Offices. These are plain white, folded-flat, 200 pounds/square inch corrugated cardboard boxes and they're cheap! These are sizes and prices from the San Francisco Bay Area. Other post offices may not have these exact sizes and prices. Check with the largest office — "main" rather than "branch."

12 x 12 x 12 inch box, with flaps folded inside, goes right onto a 1 x 12 inch shelf, helps organize and subdivide storage. Cargo of books is always ready for moving. (55 cents)

Files: Income taxes 77-80, Books on Finance

8 x 8 x 8 inches. Too small for most things except paperbacks, but ideal as shelf organizers or dividers in larger boxes. (25 cents each)

Books Novels A-E 7-80

15 x 12 x 10 inches. A good compromise if all boxes need to be the same size (for ease in carrying and stacking). (50 cents)

② Another source

for uniform, clean new boxes is moving companies. *U-Haul* is one such nationwide group. They'll sell you boxes whether or not you rent their equipment. This file box comes with a neat fold-together lid and costs about $1.50.

Several of these

can be slid under a bed for blanket, sports gear, or toy storage. On

Strong top

SKATES INFO

ICE SKATES

Hand-hold

Locking bottom

Size is 15"x 12"x 10"

Use dime-store stencil sheets to label boxes, or color code them with color paper (or cloth) spray-glued to the front face.

WINTER STUFF
·mittens, scarves
·knit caps, etc.

EXTRA SHEETS

EXTRA SHEETS

Judicious trimming with a mat knife can adapt boxes to extra low beds or couches. Cut hand-hold in lid to match covered hole.

bare wood floors cut strips of self-adhesive carpet tiles — affix to box bottoms for easy, scratch-free sliding.

Other sizes from U-Haul:

__Book Carton__: 12"x 12"x 18"
 (Double thickness.)
__Utility Carton__:
 18"x 18"x 18"
__Wardrobe Carton__:
 24"x 21"x 48" (These make fine extra closets for kids' rooms.)
__Dish Pak__: 18"x 18"x 27"
__Dish Pak cell partition kit.__

③ Ask a cabinetmaker...

drawers are about the hardest thing to get right, and therefore the most time-consuming thing to build. Short-cut this problem by using boxes for drawers. Take this three-drawer chest/nightstand for example. I built it when my son was still in diapers. Overall dimensions will depend on the sizes of your boxes.

Glue and clamp

Drawer supports

Screws and glue.

Cardboard box. (Need three.)

Finishing nails and glue. (Pre-drill holes.)

The chest uses **frame and panel** construction. Framing is 1"x 1" clear pine or redwood, except for drawer supports which are 1"x 2". Panels are 1/8" *Masonite*, painted or left natural. Drawer fronts are *Masonite* contact cemented to box ends and painted. Knobs are glued-on short lengths of dowel.

A young couple I know moved so often during one period of their lives that they simply didn't unpack. When I visited them in their San Francisco apartment, one whole wall of the living room was given over to stacked and labeled apple and orange boxes. Inside was everything they owned except cooking utensils and the clothes they were wearing.

I got to thinking that it was a smart way to live; why unpack anything until you need it — you might find you never do. The only drawbacks to this couple's system were 1: the dismal aesthetics, and 2: the difficulty of getting into the boxes. The solution: wooden boxes with the openings facing out.

First, determine a box size. A cube of about 16" x 16" x 16" seems right to me. Anything smaller won't accomodate portable TV and stereo equipment, records, and the largest of books. For paperbacks, stacks of dishes, and other small items the cube can be subdivided.

Ready-made particle board cubes are sold in unfinished furniture shops. There are two severe drawbacks: 1, dizziness, headaches, and other allergic reactions have been traced to formaldehyde gas given off by the bonding agents in particle boards. And 2, particle board is just too heavy to be moving a lot.

Plywood has (so far) not been implicated in the particle board scare. It is also lighter and stronger. Unfortunately, this comes at a price.

One way to keep plywood costs under control and still have adequate strength is to

A cube 16" on a side is usually big enough for turntable or receiver.

Use white glue and staples for fast assembly. Staple from the plywood into the boards. Only two sides need to be framed completely.

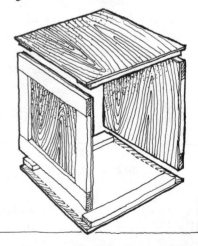

do as the crate builders do: Use the thinnest plywood — usually ⅛", Phillipine mahogany. Then frame the edges with ½" to ¾" x 2"to4" softwood. With some scrounging and nail-pulling you can get all of this material from existing crates. (See p150.)

Add a panel to the back of your boxes for extra stability and make a removable panel for the front. When faced with a move pad the spaces around the contents of each box, nail on the front panel and go.

Now here are some ways to use the boxes: The possibilities are wide open. ✒

Working Storage

If you have a hallway or a wall in a garage or basement you can work in a workbench and have storage space too. My original system and the derivation you see here was built around the pear box — a fixture for many years of the West Coast produce trade. These great little 12 by 19 by 9 inch high boxes were made of solid wood and were just the right size for tools, paint cans, spare parts, and other accouterments of my collector's life.

The pear boxes are collector's items now, but fortunately a similar size cardboard box is available, so the system still works.

All pieces of the system are modular. The

Fiberboard Boxes
12 x 15 x 10 inches high
Sears: Pkg of 4, $8.99

Letter-size drawers. Double-wall construction. Plastic drawer pull. Off-white finish. 12 x 24 x 10 inches high.
(Sears) Package of 12, unassembled, $49.99.

Top row of boxes, (lids removed for easy access) is used for tools, paints, plumbing supplies, etc; things you need regularly.
Bottom row (with lids) is for more permanent storage.

leg units are the only elements that don't come apart. They are assembled from 2 by 2s (in my workbench they are clear fir recycled from my former window settee — p. 86) and fastened with white glue and lag screws.

The shelves are 1 by 12 inch softwood cut to fit around the uprights. My benchtop is $1\frac{1}{2}$ inch plywood — a leftover from another project. It's a good, heavy work surface but it's also a pain to move. I'd suggest a piece of inexpensive $\frac{3}{4}$ inch plywood with $\frac{1}{8}$ inch untempered hardboard nailed on top to smooth out the surface.

On your right is a workbench and tool storage locker for the space with no space. The drawing shows a steel, manufactured-unit from J.C. Penney.

It will set you back about 150 dollars for the whole package, (not including the tools, of course). Folded, it's 24 by 71 by 7 inches deep. Opened out, the work table extends out 3 feet into the room.

It's a bit pricey and heavy (100 lbs.) to be an unqualified nomadic success. But suppose you only use it as a model for your own version.

You could, for example, substitute 2 x 3s or 2 x 4s for the framing members, use $\frac{1}{8}$ inch pegboard for the back panel, and 2 by 2s for the legs. Make the bottom unit separate for easier portability. 🐌

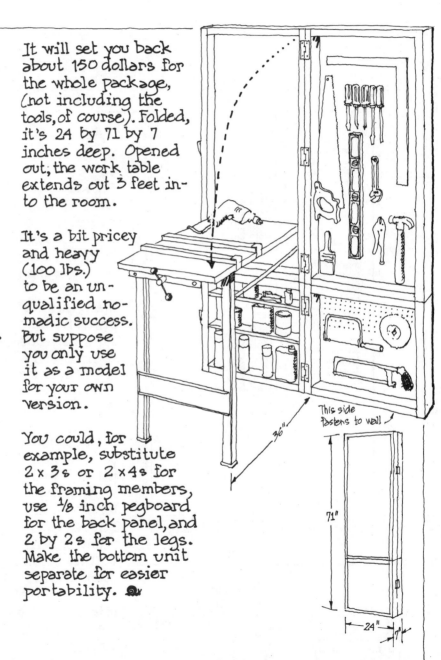

This side fastens to wall

36"

71"

24"

7"

SHAKER WALLS

This clearance is right for medium-size hardcovers & paperbacks.

This is right for large format hardcovers, paperbacks, & magazines.

Widest book determines depth of shelf.

10½" — 11½"

10¼"

10¼"

12"

12"

21½"

New 1 x 8" baseboard over (or in place of) existing one
Black out (if necessary)

¼" x 3" lag screw into studs

3/8"

Drill and countersink 1½" #10 wood screws.
Wood filler.

A friend, examining a bookshelf I'd built, decided I must be a born-again Shaker. "Believers," according to the laws of that American sect, "may not manufacture any articles which are superfluously wrought, and which have a tendency to feed the pride and vanity of man."

Well, it's not true that I gave up decoration, fancy joinery, or exotic woods for religious reasons. Instead, I seem to have come to a similar style from a different starting point: I like the simplicity and integrity of solid wood. Price usually dictates pine, so I've learned to appreciate it. Dovetail joints are out because I don't own the special power tool attachments, and I'm impatient with hand chiseling. And finally, having sorted through and selected boards with handsome grain patterns, I'm not inclined to cover them with paint or heavy stains. If what I end up with has something in common with Shaker craftsmanship, then I'm pleased. It's an indication that honesty and simplicity may be a surer way to delight the eye than all that is "superfluously wrought."

Severe limitations (even self-imposed) can stimulate creativity. Shaker humility gave birth to invention in many ways, and one of the most ingenious is their use of walls as an extension of the furnishings. By the simple device of a peg-studded wood molding running around the room at just less than door-height, the wall was made into a kind of open closet. Clothes were hung on the regularly spaced pegs; mirrors, clocks, candle sconces, bookshelves, and even chairs were also stored this way.

What you see on these pages has a spiritual, if not a literal link to Shaker practice. The peg rail has turned into a ledger, and instead of pegs I use L brackets.

The shelf unit is modest enough. Cutting dadoes ③ in the uprights will add some Shaker authenticity. However, a carefully-sawn butt joint will be nearly as strong when screwed and glued, and it's far simpler to make.

Once you have the basics on Shaker-style shelf-building you can go on to do a few variations. I built my Shaker shelves in modular units of two by six feet. They're still doing fine after five moves. ❧

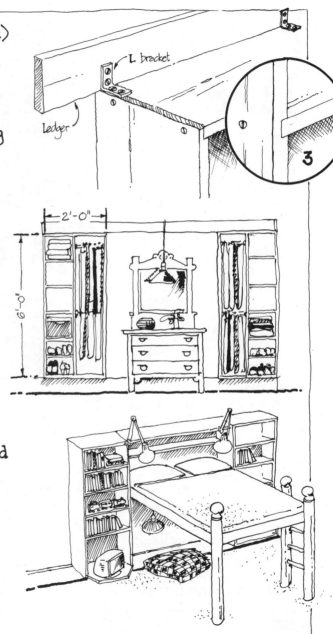

L bracket

Ledger

3

2'-0"

6'-0"

CRATE IDEAS

At a recent home show a delightful husband and wife team demonstrated the making of bread boards, knife storage blocks, and other furnishings from exotic hardwoods which they had gotten for nothing. Every month or so they simply drive their camper to a San Francisco peninsular motorcycle import center and load up with the slats and 2 x 4s from discarded packing crates. They laminate the pieces together using random lengths and thicknesses with an eye toward a collage of wood types and colors. When sanded and varnished the results are lovely, and free!

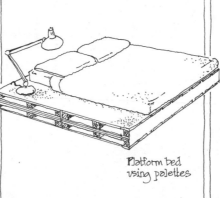

Platform bed using palettes

A **Palette** is a type of crate used to raise a stack of merchandise just off the ground so the tines of a fork lift can slip under it. Palettes are sturdy but crude and they are commonly left lying about behind grocery stores and other high volume retail outlets. You can ask, or you can just act. I'd say you're within the bounds of propriety if you take obviously damaged palettes or others that are clearly not being used. (I will not, however, be liable for your bail.)

Palettes can be used to lift your load, too— especially to raise a bed to a new level or to visually separate a dining area from the rest of the room.

More Crate Ideas:

OUR UNION

is a brand of San Joaquin Valley*asparagus. Their crates have artful labels and a curious wider-at-the-bottom shape. Could this be simply because bunches of asparagus bulge at the bottom too?

Whatever the explanation, this crate (or a similar one) is well worth the scavenging. With some modification,** it becomes a very nifty desk-top file box.

(1) Begin by carefully removing all the slats:

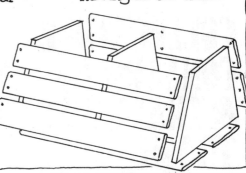

(2) Discard the bottom slats and the center divider. (These make good scrap-wood for kid's building projects.) Cut an equal amount off both ends of all side slats so as to make them 13¼ inches long.

This helps eliminate some nail holes and any damaged ends:

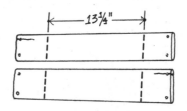

|← 13¼" →|

(3) Now cut a new, solid bottom for the box from a scrap of ¼" to ½" plywood, chipboard or what-have-you. (It won't show.) The dimensions for this are 11 inches (check against the width of your crate) by 12 inches.

(4) Assemble the new bottom and the original box ends:

White glue

Box nails

(5) Then replace the slats using brads. (Drill pilot holes first.) Or use a staple gun and 9/16" staples. Lightly round all rough edges with sandpaper.

(6) Drop in a package of letter-size file folders and get organized, with style.

---

* That's California, of course, but the crates are shipped all over the country (and the world). Try small specialty food markets, and if at first you don't succeed... use a cantaloupe crate instead!

**For some reason these step-by-step instructions make this project look complicated. It's not. Once you've scored a crate, the rest is simple.

COLLECTABLE CONTAINERS & TRACTABLE TRASH

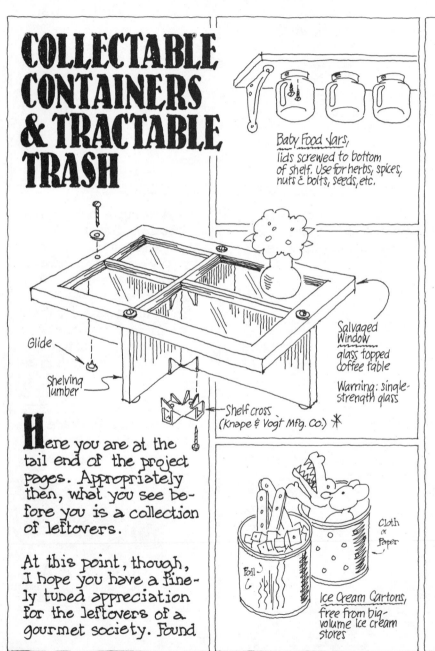

Baby Food Jars, lids screwed to bottom of shelf. Use for herbs, spices, nuts & bolts, seeds, etc.

Glide

Shelving lumber

Salvaged Window glass topped coffee table

Warning: single-strength glass

Shelf cross (Knape & Vogt Mfg. Co.) ✳

Foil

Cloth or Paper

Ice Cream Cartons, free from big-volume ice cream stores

Here you are at the tail end of the project pages. Appropriately then, what you see before you is a collection of leftovers.

At this point, though, I hope you have a finely tuned appreciation for the leftovers of a gourmet society. Found and recycled materials are a part of many projects in the book, and I've tried all along to make the distinction between "leftovers" and "garbage."

Some of the projects on these pages ask you to look with new eyes at your own throwaways: jars, cans, boxes, worn-out clothes. Others suggest that you be alert to new uses for industrial discards.

Either way you save energy: 1) by recycling; 2) by reducing your need for new materials; and 3) by lowering the world total of garbage trucks.

But the central idea is to have some fun. Finding a new use for a familiar object takes playfulness and whimsy. So, be my guest. Indulge your fantasies and demonstrate your independence from the status quo. 🐾

Tool holders using band cut from _Old Inner Tube_

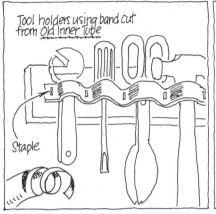

Staple

5 Gallon Olive Oil or Rice Vinegar Tins from restaurants

RICE VINEGAR

Cardboard Barrels in various sizes, free from manufacturers who use chemical products that come packed in these (inquire about toxic residues).

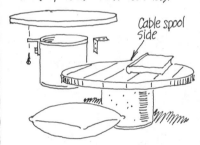

Cable spool side

Large Wool Socks (various patterns)

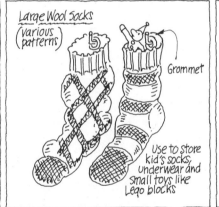

Grommet

Use to store kid's socks, underwear and small toys like Lego blocks

Large Juice Cans for cubbies (box found or made to fit, see p. 142-145)

Cedar Blocks sold in bundles as firewood

Big Plastic Wastebaskets cut in half and staple to 1 X 1 s, screw to back of closet door. Use for sorting and storing dirty clothes.

Wall-hung row of Designer Shopping Bags

CON RAN'S
MACY'S

Cut off one handle. Cut cardboard to spread bottom.

Leases, Rental Agreements, and The Moveable Nest

On the table in front of me is a two-hundred-page book on tenant's rights—just for California! Its preface cautions that the book is still not enough to entirely supplant the need for a lawyer. The question arises: What can I possibly hope to do, in the next few pages, that will be useful in California, and in the rest of the country as well?

I've only got one answer for that: After reading this section, you'll be better informed than *I* was in the majority of my rental deals. I can't promise that you'll be a match for an unscrupulous owner*, but you *will* have your antennae raised. Connecting with these subjects, however briefly, should help sensitize you about where you are well-informed, and where you need to ask some questions.

Keep in mind that this discussion covers owner/tenant agreements only as they pertain to maintenance and alterations. These are the areas of law that have direct bearing on how and to what extent you build your own moveable nest.

*Here, and throughout this section, I'll use "owner" as a gender-free substitute for the unwieldly "landlord/land-lady."

Is It a Lease, or a Leash?

I am about to join the chorus of lawyers, legal aid societies, and realtors who predict dire consequences for any tenant who doesn't have a written rental agreement or a lease. But first I have a pertinent confession to make.

My present lease, now three years old, is the first such written agreement I've had. That means eight previous rentals were all based on a short talk and a handshake. It's fine when they work, and these did. But they were intimate, small-scale arrangements with owners of private homes, duplexes, and the like.

Three new developments changed my attitude toward "getting it in writing." One is the business orientation of my present landlord. He owns some twenty properties and obviously does not concern himself with each tenant individually. Also the market has changed. Turnover of rentals is slow in this area, and good places are hard to find. I wanted some guarantee that I could stay for a while, and without arbitrary rent increases. (A lease usually fixes the rent for the life of the agreement, typically a year. A rental agreement is a month-to-month arrangement, thirty days being sufficient legal notice of a rent hike.) My third reason for signing up was that the landlord didn't give me a choice.

Marriage vows don't prevent divorce. And rental contracts cannot prevent disagreement. The best use of a contract, and I say this after many dealings with trustworthy people, with and without documents, is that by writing it down, you are forced to confront potentially troublesome issues *while you are still agreeable*. It's like making a grocery list, leaving it at home, but remembering what to get anyway, just because you had written it once. The *process* of making a contract is the important part. Work from a preprinted form, or make your own list. Discuss. Make eye contact. Write it, sign and date it, and shake on it. In many cases, with this kind of face-to-face meeting, you will never need to refer to the contract again.

A Balancing Act

Normally, I'm a mild-mannered believer in the "you

156

scratch my back, I'll scratch yours" school of owner/tenant relations. But there is one kind of problem that has the power to unbalance all my cooperative instincts and turn me into an ogre ... *stopped-up drains.* Is this a widespread complaint, I wonder, or does it just follow *me* around? Three different rentals in a row have had some variety of drainage/sewer difficulties. Well, if this is my karma, at least I'm beginning to see some signs of change.

I mark the beginning of the transformation with my most recent clogged-drain battle. In the same week, first the toilet, then the sink, then the shower backed up. I applied all remedies—rubber plungers, liquid drain openers, a wire snake. I really extended myself beyond the call of ten-ant duty. This is not just too much toilet paper, I thought. This proves that the whole system is blocked, and it's going to take at least dynamite. This is a job for a professional.

Well, Roto-Rooter billed my landlord the thirty-two dollars, but just between you, me, and the repairman, all the standing water went merrily down the drain as soon as we removed the grate from the floor of the shower. It seems that between the grate and the extra metal strainer I had so conscientiously added to trap hair, a thick film of soap had formed, and first slowed, then eventually almost stopped the flow of water. The slowness in the other drains had mysteriously ended. It *wasn't* one monumental problem; only several little ones. So now there's a new entry in that big mental notebook I call "Being Cautious about Crying Wolf."

Why this reluctance to call for help? Some people are going to think this is pretty strange behavior for a renter; especially if they're like my neighbor, who calls the owner in to change the furnace filter. I realize that some tenants avoid doing maintenance as a matter of principle. They're seeing a lot of money go into rent, with no equity, no tax benefits in return. So they become determined to get all that they can squeeze out of their disappearing payments. They look upon rent as a monthly fee for a service—housing, and all the maintenance that goes with it. And it makes sense, for them.

I'm after something quite different. I'm after the *feeling,* if not the fact of ownership. Calling in the maintenance crew, to do something I can do myself, takes away some of my power. As a first concession, I have to plan to be at home on the days when the workers will be there. In the case of replacing some leaking storm gutters (something I clearly couldn't handle myself), the process stretched out to more than a month. I kept calling. They kept saying they were working on it.

Of course, I could simply be away from home, let the maintenance people enter with a passkey, and come home to find the problem, hopefully, solved. But this, I calculate, is an even higher price to pay for service: I give up my sense of competence *and* my privacy. If I repair a

dripping faucet, I become familiar with it, and it becomes more clearly mine. If I never touch the job—if it is done while I'm gone, by the owner's unseen agent—then that faucet, the sink, maybe even the bathroom are partly lost to me. They move closer to the owner's domain.

I will gladly concede to him the drainpipes. But I will not give up the bathroom!

There is another reason not to give away the responsibility for minor maintenance. Landlord*/tenant law has its basis in feudalism. It worked like this: The lord of the manor, by his leave, lent you a small parcel of his holdings. Your

*The masculine form for historical realism.

obligation was to farm it wisely and well and give him a portion of your harvest (rent). In return, he agreed to protect your (his) farm from any real or imagined threat: great hairy beasts, or other greedy lords of the land who would just as leave have your farm, and maybe you, counted in *their* holdings. Note the paternalism. It's a protection racket. The Godfather will provide, provided you have been good to the Godfather.

Now, don't think this historical precedent has been lost on today's patriarchs. A hard look at any standard lease will reveal how the owner still has the upper hand. You are there pretty much at the owner's sufferance. The sacrosanct rights of private property are extended to the owner, not to you. From the

158

traditional, legal point of view, you have taken charge of a code-approved, legal rental unit. If something goes wrong, it's probably due to "tenant neglect." It's an awful presumption, but it's there. And there are just enough tenant horror stories (some true) to keep the myth alive.

Now look at your complaints from this perspective. The more times you run to papa owner crying over little cuts and bruises, and the more times he has to call in a high-priced specialist when all that's really needed is a Band-aid, the more he's going to start focusing attention on this one, to him, far from ideal tenant.

And now that you have drawn this attention (for whatever good and legitimate reasons), you'd better hope that your own hands are clean. Suppose the owner suddenly takes notice of the holes you drilled for your shelving system. Did you ever ask? And what about the new color of the kitchen? Didn't you sign a lease that said you wouldn't paint without written permission? Well, you get the idea. Pickiness breeds pickiness. Or, more positively stated, if you are generous in your responsibility for the minor aches and pains, you're banking goodwill and fairness which will shine in your favor when you really do need help. *And,* you will give yourself the widest possible latitude in which to make your rented place feel like your own.

Comes the Revolution

So much for the lesson in tenant diplomacy. The actual statutes are changing. Since the beginning of the sixties consumers have fought and won many cases in favor of the rights of tenants. Unfortunately, many of these important precedents are scattered about in volumes of case reports and statute books. The law changes slowly enough; the even bigger delay is in the process of informing those people whose rights have been affected. An owner brandishing a form lease may be offering you an out-of-date document full of illegal and unfair clauses. Regrettably, your signature on that document gives it the presumption of law. Should there be subsequent litigation, the illegal clauses would probably be held invalid by the courts, but there is no remedy for your having agreed to an unfair clause.

Are you convinced that ignorance is no excuse, and that there is much to be ignorant about? Good. Go directly to the library and get *The Rights of Tenants, An American Civil Liberties Handbook,* by Richard E. Blumberg and James R. Grow (Avon Books, 1978). Its readable, direct, question-and-answer format will bring you up to date on all aspects of your legal position as a tenant, nationwide. Highly recommended.

Deeper into the Lease

Short of reading *The Rights of Tenants,* there are a few things you should know about lease language that may immediately affect your remodeling plans.

Here, for example, is the pertinent section of *my* lease, which I signed, in full possession of my faculties. It's a standard printed form that owners and agents use all over the country. The date of the last revision is August 1979.

> MAINTENANCE, REPAIRS OR ALTERATIONS: Tenant acknowledges that the premises are in good order and repair, unless otherwise indicated herein. Owner may at any time give tenant a written inventory of furniture and furnishings on the premises and Tenant shall be deemed to have possession of all said furniture and furnishings in good condition and repair, unless he objects thereto in writing within five days [!—ed.] after receipt of such inventory.

And this paragraph goes on. I just want you to notice how, even with the first sentence, the initiative is given to the owner. "Tenant acknowledges that the premises are in good order and repair. . . ." How do you *know* they are? One thing is for sure, you don't wait for the landlord to send you an inventory. You march right in with note pad, pencil, and if possible, a camera, and you make your *own* inventory. Note all furniture and fixtures along with specifics about the condition of each, e.g.: "L. R. carpet—dark stain in N.E. corner." Photographs are really helpful in showing worn carpeting or the general condition of a wood floor. Get the owner to sign and date your inventory (and the photos, if any).

Sounds like a lot of work? It is. But your freedom to make extensive changes is ethically and often legally conditional upon your putting everything back the way you found it. A sizable security deposit may also be at stake. The inventory is your guarantee that one, two, three years down the road, both you and the owner will have similar memories of how things were when you moved in.

The lease continues:

> Tenant shall, at his own expense, and at all times, maintain the premises in a clean and sanitary manner including all equipment, appliances, furniture and furnishings therein and shall surrender the same, at termination hereof, in as good condition as received, normal wear and tear excepted.

"Normal wear and tear" is obviously a judgment. If you have kids and/or pets, or if you're planning to use one bedroom for karate instruction, a set of "before" photographs is good insurance, in case the owner decides later that your use was unusually taxing. Photos can also work as a diplomatic lever—evidence in advance of your good intentions.

> Tenant shall be responsible for damages caused by his negligence and that of his family or invitees or guests. Tenant shall not paint, paper, or otherwise redecorate or make alterations to the premises without the prior written consent of the owner.

Ah, there in that last sentence is the catchall. You'll certainly have to play that one by ear. Repainting in the same or a similar color should not raise any hackles. (My landlord gave me verbal permission to paint any walls so long as I painted them white.) I also don't hesitate to remove doors, replace light fixtures, attach shelves, or do any other work that can be conscientiously undone when I move.

You should be aware, however, that some state laws (California is one), specify that anything which is nailed, screwed, or bolted to the premises becomes the property of the owner. (Feudalism again?) The simple, sure way around this is to get written permission before you attach things like shelves, cupboards, room dividers, and possibly even air conditioners and stereo speakers. Be certain the agreement clearly states that you will be removing these items when you go, and that the owner waives any claims he or she may have upon them. You, in turn, will need to assure that you will repair any damage caused by the mounting hardware.

Whenever you're debating whether or not to get permission, keep in mind that though an owner may accept or take no notice of your modifications on a routine visit, the ultimate test comes when it's time to refund the security deposit. You can choose to live with that uncertainty, or you can get everything in writing.

Overdoing It Yourself

There is a possible drawback to being the kind of conscientious, responsible tenant that I'm promoting: An owner may see how independent you are and decide that you don't need any attention at all. This happened to me in a cozy bungalow I rented in Berkeley. I fixed faucets, painted, even puttied windows, but when the roof began to leak, I drew the line and called the owner. He began to make suggestions about where I could get the materials until my hasty interjection cleared up the mystery of where my responsibility ended. He saw my point, but didn't make haste to come and fix the roof.

Faced with such a laissez-faire owner, you may be tempted to fix the thing yourself. If it's cut and dried, a new toilet flush valve, for example, you might just get the owner to agree to pay for the parts and fix it yourself. No harm in asking for some compensation for your labor as well. With one trusting owner, who lived far away, I had permission to do anything needed and take expenses and a small charge for my labor off the rent. Such arrangements are possible, and point up the value of approaching the owner in a way that allows him or her to be open and flexible. The old mutual back-scratching game again.

But what if being reasonable doesn't get you anywhere? The owner refuses to make repairs or procrastinates to the same effect. Can you go ahead and make the repairs, or have them made, and deduct the expense from next month's rent? The answer is a qualified "yes." This "repair and deduct" remedy is part of most state laws. But it only covers certain defects, usually related to health or safety—plumbing failures, lighting and wiring problems, heating, and so on. You must notify the owner (preferably in writing) and you must allow a "reasonable time" for a response. A broken water heater needs

162

action in a few days; an inoperable furnace is not as urgent in June as in January. (Thirty days is considered reasonable for non-emergencies.) If there is no response, you have the right to make the repairs yourself or to hire a specialist. The itemized costs, including your time, can be deducted from the next month's rent. In California you cannot deduct repairs amounting to more than one month's rent, and you cannot use this remedy more than twice in any twelve-month period.

That's a somewhat sketchy description of a fairly complicated procedure. Since state laws vary, you had best contact a local attorney or legal aid office for help if you decide to go this way. The real point of the discussion is that this legal recourse, like most legal remedies, is involved and time-consuming. It is there as a last resort. But your life will be easier if you spend the time at the beginning of your rental searches, finding reasonable owners, asking all your questions, and arriving at a relationship of trust through the working out of a mutually acceptable lease or rental agreement.

The Point

Do as I say; not as I've done. I'm a new recruit to the world of leases, but a firm believer. Face-to-face discussions, promises, and handshakes are the peanut butter of a rental arrangement, the lease is the toast. 🐌

Shopping Lists

Obviously I haven't hesitated to use myself as an example in this book. By using my "I," and my hand lettering, I hoped to emphasize that what you're getting is personal—maybe a little idiosyncratic—but definitely real, lived-in stuff. I also hoped to demystify the design and selection process so that you would not feel separated from it all and might be tempted to disagree, alter, or otherwise take these ideas and make them yours.

In this section the gaps widen.

The material becomes sketchier, the suggestions more general. The intention is the same, only more so. You *were* getting the guided tour; now you're in the driver's seat. Soon you won't need this vehicle at all.

Stalking the Yellow Pages

Even the casual do-it-your-selfer must be aware that hardware stores are no longer the variety palaces of even a few years back. Merchandise has been standardized. There are fewer sizes, and unique specialty items—slow movers—have been dropped. In some large metropolitan areas there has been a conscious effort to revive the fully equipped comprehensive hardware store, usually catering expressly to do-it-yourselfers. This is encouraging, and mail order is another option. But probably you can vary your hardware diet right in your own hometown, simply by shopping in retail outlets you might not think of as hardware stores. Here are a few for starters, plus an item or two to show why it's worth

going there. Check your Yellow Pages under these headings for sources in your locale.

Ship Chandlers and Boat Shops. Sometimes these are the only places to find brass hardware. Brass sash pulls and finger latches add a craftsmanly finishing touch to your project without too much trouble or expense. Also check for maritime signal flags, and state and nation flags, for use as decorative window or wall coverings and bedspreads.

Craft and Hobby Stores. While big hardware manufacturers are streamlining their product offerings, the suppliers of hobby and craft specialties seem to be going in just the opposite direction. These cottage industries can apparently thrive, or at least survive, selling small quantities of many unique items. The retail outlets for these products are great places to browse. I look for unusual fasteners, specialty adhesives and paints, wood turnings, and metal rings. I'm more likely to use what I find as inspiration for a new project, than to seek out a specific solution. Sometimes it's a little of each, as with this embroidery hoop which appeared just at the time I was trying to fit some wide-topped industrial glass shades to much smaller hanging sockets. The adjustable hoop, minus its inner ring, provided an elegant solution.

Sporting Goods Stores.
You'll probably find me in the fishing tackle department. That's where I get spools of nylon leader, which is perfect for hanging picture frames and other objects. This almost clear yet exceptionally strong thread will take on the color of your wall and virtually disappear. This is also the place to get snap swivels, nifty brass hooks with a rotating section

that allows lures to turn freely on fishing lines. I use them as a neat way to attach curtains to sliding rings.

Wall and ceiling hangers are usually rated in maximum pounds of holding strength. This is helpful *if* you know what your hang*ees* (plants, pictures, and so on) weigh. A fishing scale, like the *Zebco DeLiar,* is an inexpensive and reasonably accurate tool for measurements in the useful zero-to-28 pounds range.

Still in the sporting goods store but now in the camping supplies department, look for chrome-plated cookout grills. These are remarkably inexpensive, and, clamped or wired together in box shapes, or bracketed from walls as shelves, they make neat open storage units.

See also p.127

Concrete Supplies. That's the heading in the Yellow Pages, but it doesn't tell the whole story. You'll be looking for a place that sells all kinds of masonry supplies, including brick, concrete block, and drain tile. A fairly big yard will have a number of drain tiles and concrete blocks that will be much more interesting than the limited selection found in lumberyards. With a wider choice, you can ring some nice changes on the old reliable concrete-block shelving unit.

Do-It-Yourself Frame Shops.

Here's where I found a wall hanger that I'd never seen in a hardware store. Its name is *Floreat Hanger* and it's rated at 75 pounds! The secret of its great holding strength seems to be the three extra-sharp steel pins that are guided into the wall by extra long angled

throats built into the hanger body. These German imports are pricey—almost a dollar for the 75-pound model. Smaller ones are also available. For really heavy picture hanging on plasterboard they may be worth the ticket.

Framing shops are also a likely source for picture rail hangers, which are sometimes scarce in hardware stores.

There is no end to this. Once you start watching for unusual hardware it will begin to appear in all kinds of places. Here are some other sources

that I've found fruitful:

Restaurant Suppliers
Tack Shops
Mountaineering Equipment
   Stores
Government Surplus Outlets
Scuba Diving Shops
Tent and Awning Makers
Plumbing and Heating
   Suppliers

The Older, the Better

If you're willing to spend a little extra time shopping (you could think of it as entertainment), it's possible to avoid hardware stores and retail lumber outlets and still get most of the supplies you need. The magic word is "used." Suddenly prices go down, but quality may well go up. You'll be at the receiving end of an established truth: "They don't make 'em like that anymore." With lumber, hardware, and hand tools, the cliché comes true.

Lumber, Used, and *Building Materials, Used.* Those are the headings to look for in the Yellow Pages. Be prepared to borrow a truck or van and drive to the outskirts. The best bargains are not in the high-rent district. But it's worth the journey to find 2 × 4s that are actually two inches by four inches, not to mention dry and straight (the split and checked material doesn't survive the salvage operation). Plywood at half price, plastic laminates (for countertops), old doors (for tabletops), and old windows (to hang in front of your plain new windows), these are things to keep an eye out for. Old nails are the drawback to old lumber. Most of the visible nails have been removed, but don't try to run used lumber through a planer to smooth it up, unless you're prepared to pay for the damage a buried nail can do to a twenty-dollar planer blade.

Not so far from home is the damaged-lumber pile—"the boneyard"—at your local lumber dealer. You may have to ask about this; it's not often advertised. Sometimes it's just the place they put unsalable merchandise. Prices are most often quite negotiable, beginning at free, and going up. But don't expect to bargain at eleven A.M. Saturday morning. Pick a time when regular business is slow and the salespeople have time to be friendly and accommodating.

Another little-publicized lumberyard bargain is called the "farmer's load." It's a bundle of mixed-dimensional lumber, perhaps 2 × 4s, 2 × 6s, 2 × 8s, and 2 × 10s, in "short ends" (cutoffs from longer pieces), and other odd lengths, but otherwise in good condition.

Pickets ripped from odd lengths (farmer's load).

You pay one price, usually less than half of retail, if you carry away the entire bundle. (Not too long ago a ten-dollar farmer's load was more than I could carry in one trip with my small station wagon.) Farmer's loads are an occasional kind of find, but you may *never* find one if you don't ask. I have one or two acquaintances at each lumberyard whom I regularly chat with. They can usually tell me about damaged shipments, upcoming sales, and other bargains: good people to know.

Good hand tools develop a patina and friendliness with age. As with used lumber, the tools that are going to break have already broken. The survivors are the tried and true, already broken in, and smoothly fitting the hand.

Popular as they are, they are also very available. Flea markets are the most dependable source. At our local flea there are several regular dealers who specialize in tools. You can also watch for estate sales in the want ads. If you have a local "pay only if your item sells" advertising tabloid, by all means check it out for tools *and* lumber.

All the old handyman types seem to be hoarders of vast collections of assorted hardware. I wonder if they ever have to shop for anything. The mystery is, how to get such a collection *started*. Mine is growing just by frugal saving of the remnants of "blister packs." I no longer throw a fit at having to buy a package of seven screws when I only need four. The extras become part of my "stores." Some time ago a local hardware store was selling out all their broken packages and remnants. I bought the whole scrambled tray of stuff for six dollars, and spent many happy, therapeutic hours sorting this jumble into baby-food jars. Smaller-scale deals like this can be found at garage sales and flea markets.

The last source I'll mention is the hardest to describe. It can be a treasure trove of lumber, hardware, and even furniture, but it's only available to those who can step outside some habits of perception. We are so conditioned to neatly stacked, shrink-wrapped, color-coded, and price-marked merchandise, that when something appears in a different context we're not likely to realize it's both useful and available. I'm talking about *junk,* or more correctly, that which someone else considers useless. Once you develop the habits of looking and asking, valuable castoffs are everywhere. You may experience some embarrass-

170

ment at first (scavenging is freighted with all kinds of negative images), but this is offset by an occasional "find"—a paneled door; a brass soap dish sleeping under five layers of paint; or something else that you couldn't have come upon any other way. You get a taste of playing by different rules; a feeling that your sheer cleverness has brought you the unheard of—something for nothing.

Some fruitful scavenging can be done in debris boxes, especially where remodeling is going on. The really good stuff is often only hinted at by the box out front. There may be other items stacked around the site that will be hauled away if no one asks. A small cash offering could be helpful.

Alleys are worth exploring for less-organized dumping. These are likely places to find motorcycle crates (some exotic hardwoods are used in the imported ones), as well as other types of wooden boxes. Return trips or questioning may disclose the trash pickup day. The most lucrative time to make your call may be just ahead of the *paid* scavengers.

Frustration may result from making detailed plans, then seeking used materials to carry them out. Try gathering the materials first, letting the shapes and sizes of what you find influence the final design. Happy hunting!

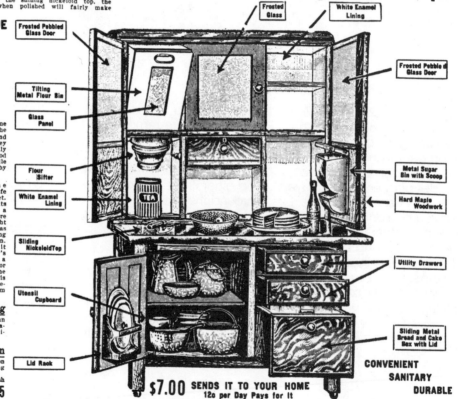

As Near as Your Mailbox

If my home were a business, I would be the highest-ranking employee. In that light, does it make sense for me to also be the chief gofer? Of course I can learn a lot in my shopping excursions—there's no substitute for handling the real material. But when it's important for me to be at home rather than out looking for a parking place, I use an energy-saving device that's older than the automobile—mail order. Not only do my suppliers do the driving; they also parade before me—via illustrated catalogs—a variety of goods I couldn't hope to see in a month of shopping. I can sit at my desk, my drawing pad, tape measure, and coffee cup within easy reach, and have access to the largest or the most specialized warehouses in the country.

I have direct experience with many of the following companies. Others are suppliers for merchandise which I usually obtain locally, but which may be hard to find away from big cities. An asterisk indicates a manufacturer who does not normally do mail order but can supply catalogs or brochures and direct you to a local supplier. In any case, my experience is not your experience.

All-Purpose Mail Order

If you're willing to search, some surprisingly good, honest workmanship is available from Sears and other "supermarket" mail order catalogs. Ask about special catalog supplements: Tools and Hardware; RV and Mobile Homes; Farm and Garden; etc.

Conran's
145 Huguenot St.
New Rochelle, NY 10801
Catalog $2
High tech and simple pine furniture, contemporary lighting fixtures, sheets, floor coverings, kitchen gear, all selected with a designer's eye. Buy, or be inspired to build, your own version.

The Cumberland General Store Wish & Want Book
The Cumberland General Store
Route 3
Crossville, TN 38555
Homestead-oriented merchandise, the great stuff you may have thought wasn't made anymore.

J. C. Penney
Circulation Department
Box 2056
Milwaukee, WI 53201
Catalog $2,
redeemable on first purchase.

Montgomery Ward & Co.
Check your phone book under Montgomery Ward, catalog sales, and ask for nearest mail order headquarters.
In the West write to:
Montgomery Ward & Co.
2825 East 14th St.
Oakland, CA 94616
Catalog $2,
redeemable on first purchase.

Sears, Roebuck and Co.
Check your phone book under Sears or write for location of nearest mail order plant to:
Sears, Roebuck and Co.
925 South Homan Ave.
Chicago, IL 60607
Catalog $2,
redeemable on first purchase.

The Wholesale by Mail Catalog
Prudence McCullogh, Editor
1979, 203 pages
$5.95 postpaid
St. Martin's Press, Inc.
175 Fifth Ave.
New York, NY 10010
350 sources of mail order goods, 30% to 90% off list price.

Accessories

Edmund Scientific Co.
3885 Edscorp Building
Barrington, NJ 08007
Catalog $1
A great catalog of scientific toys and tools. Kids love it.

L. L. Bean, Inc.
1580 Birch St.
Freeport, ME 04033
Pine kitchen tool holders.

The Nature Company
P.O. Box 7137
Berkeley, CA 94707
Prisms and other light-changing devices. Catalog free.

Williams-Sonoma
5750 Hollis St.
Emeryville, CA 94608

Fabrics

Jensen-Lewis
156 Seventh Ave.
New York, NY 10011
Heavy canvas in 28 colors.
Lightweight canvas in 12 colors.

Also a source for counter-height director's chairs.

*Marimekko
7 West 56th St.
New York, NY 10019

Voice of the Mountains
(The Vermont Country Store Catalog)
The Vermont Country Store
Weston, VT 05161
An extensive collection of Early American calico, $1.99 per yard, 36" wide, and many other solid, country-bred items.

Fasteners

*Imperial Fastener Corp.
1400 Southwest 8th St.
Pompano Beach, FL 33060
Hospital ceiling track—
a neat shower-curtain solution.

*Moore Push-Pin Co.
1300 East Mermaid Lane
Wyndmoor, PA 19118
If you can't find ⅝" pushpins or hard-surface wall fasteners locally, ask the company that makes them. They make many other interesting fasteners, too. Write for catalog.

Knope & Vogt Manufacturing Co.
2700 Oak Industrial Dr. NE
Grand Rapids, MI 49505
Shelf clips. See pp. 134, 154.

*Nicro Fico
2065 West Bay Ave. 140
San Leandro, CA 94577
Marine hardware.

Selfix, Inc.
311 West Superior St.
Chicago, IL 60610
Replacement glue capsules for repositioning Selfix self-gluing hooks. See pp. 33, 34.

Velcro U.S.A., Inc.
681 Fifth Ave.
New York, NY 10022
Rug holders, curtain hang-ups, and other special application kits using Velcro strips.

Furniture

Aerogon Industries, Inc.
Box 36462
6309 Westline Dr.
Houston, TX 77036
Good-looking contemporary and reproduction solid-wood furniture in kit form.

The Carborundum Company
Consumer Products Division
923 Old Nepperhan Ave.
Yonkers, NY 10703
Natural grain rock maple "decor decks."

Cohasset Colonials
Cohasset, MA 02025
Catalog $1
Assemble and finish simple antique furniture reproductions.

Sam Flax
55 East 55th St.
New York, NY 10022
Catalog $2
Materials for artists and drafts-persons, well designed and adaptable to other uses.

Guild of Shaker Crafts, Inc.
401 West Savidge St.
Spring Lake, MI 49456
Catalog $1.50

*Jasper Desk Co.
Box 111
Jasper, IN 47546
Schoolroom and office furniture in solid wood, the way you remember it.

*Pollard Bros. Mfg. Co., Inc.
5504 Northwest Hwy. N.
Chicago, IL 60630
Sturdy steel leg assemblies for
building your own tables.

Standard Structures Inc.
P.O. Box K
Santa Rosa, CA 95402
Laminated fir tabletops.

*The Steele Canvas Basket Co., Inc.
199 Concord Turnpike
Cambridge, MA 02140
Unique, inexpensive, fabric and
steel tables and baskets.

*Thonet
491 East Princess St.
York, PA 17403
Manufacturer of classic bentwood
furniture, lightweight and durable.

Workbench
470 Park Ave. South
New York, NY 10016
Simple, elegant, and expensive pine
furniture.

Lighting

*Abolite Lighting, Inc.
West Lafayette, OH 43845
Porcelain-enamel industrial lamp-
shades and fittings. A good selection
for hanging lamps.

*Four Star Stage Lighting
3935 North Mission Rd.
Los Angeles, CA 90031
Professional theater lighting.

*Holophane Division
Johns Manville
Greenwood Plaza
Denver, CO 80217
Good-looking industrial glass lamp-
shades.

*Halo Lighting
Division of McGraw Edison Co.
400 Busse Rd.
Elk Grove Village, IL 60007
Track lighting and accessories.

George Kovacs
831 Madison Ave.
New York, NY 10021
Contemporary lighting fixtures.

*Ledu Lamp Division
Wasomark, Inc.
1 Willard Rd.
Norwalk, CT 06851
Inexpensive versions of the Luxo
floating lamps. See p. 64.

*Luxo Lamp Corp.
Monument Park
Port Chester, NY 10573
Flexible task lighting.

*Swivelier Lighting Products Division
Nanuet, NY 10954
A complete line of track
lighting and accessories.

Arthur H. Thomas Co.
Vine Street at Third, Box 779
Philadelphia, PA 19106
Will mail order medical Luxo
lamps, laboratory glass, and
other interesting medical items.

Storage and Display

Abstracta Structures, Inc.
101 Park Ave.
New York, NY 10017
Chrome tubes and friction-fit
corner hardware make an easy-to-
assemble and easy-to-live-with
home display and storage system.

C & H Distributors, Inc.
401 South 5th St.
Milwaukee, WI 53204
Mail order nifty wood storage and
scrap material boxes. Many uses.

Darby Creek, Inc.
319 East County Line Road
Haverford, PA 19041
"Drawer on the wall" hanging
organizer of cotton duck.

Fidelity Products Co.
705 Pennsylvania Ave. So.
Minneapolis, MN 55426
Office equipment, especially
cardboard filing drawers, shelves,
flat boxes, etc. with great potential.
Also steel shelving.

The Horchow Collection
Box 34257
Dallas, TX 75234
Swing out wall-mounted storage
trays, and some other interesting
odd items. The selection changes
from season to season.

McCoy Coop Co.
P.O. Box 521
Fairfax, VA 22030
Wood chicken coops make
unique storage/display units
for books, records.

Pacific Shelving
1901 West El Segundo Blvd.
Compton, CA 90222
Steel shelving that can be
used at home.

Timberline
Box 966
25305 Cypress Ave.
Lomita, CA 90717
Wood storage units.

Tools

AMT Power Tools
American Machine and Tool Co.
Fourth and Spring Streets
Royersford, PA 19468
Low cost, compact power tools.
You build your own extension tables,
etc., from plans provided.

Gilliom Power Tool Kits
Gilliom Manufacturing Inc.
1109 North 2nd St.
St. Charles, MO 63301
Information $0.50.
Build your own power tools—
Gilliom furnishes the motor and
metal parts—you do the housing
with plywood.

Magna-Clean Window Washer
by Byco Enterprises
23052 Lake Forest Dr.
Unit G1
Laguna Hills, CA 92653
See p. 80

Mutual Hardware Corp.
5-45 49th Ave.
Long Island City, NY 11101
Catalog $1.50
Stage and scenery hardware—do
your own "stage set" and keep
it light and moveable. This is the
place to get floor paint
that peels away.

U.S. General Supply Corp.
100 General Place
Jericho, NY 11753
Catalog free.
A discount source for all brands and
qualities of tools. Good for brows-
ing—chances are there's a tool already designed for your special
needs.

Shop Talk

Here's your brief lexicon and illustrated guide to the arcane language of lumberyard and hardware store. When I first planned this section, I thought of it as a service to the real novice. Now that it's done, I'm surprised to see that it could be useful to more experienced nestbuilders as well. It brings together in one place a body of information that you might search through several reference works to find, if you were inclined to take the time. I must say that in researching this section, I found quite a few terms that I had been habitually misusing.

Approach this section just as you would a dictionary. Most of the words appear elsewhere in the book, and in a few cases the definition refers back to that context.

Any word appearing, within the definition, in **bold-face** type is also defined in "Shop Talk." Take special notice of the illustrations. In many cases the information they contain appears nowhere else in the book.

AD
Air-dried. Refers to a process for curing lumber in stacks which are sheltered from rain but open to the atmosphere. Compare **kiln-dried.**

angle iron
Fastener used to hold and/or reinforce corner joints. A **gusseted** angle iron has greater resistance to **racking.**

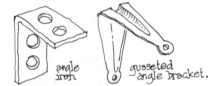

angle iron

gusseted angle bracket.

beam
A board or timber (large board), running horizontally and supporting something above, like a ceiling or floor.

bender board
A type of **milled** lumber, usually ¼" to ½" thick and 4" to 8" wide—meant for edging ("bending") around a lawn, garden plot, or walkway. Usually redwood or cedar because of their rot-resisting qualities. It is good-looking, cheap, and useful in many ways other than its intended one.

board foot
A measure of quantity. Used in pricing lumber. One board foot is defined as a **nominal**-size piece of wood 1" thick by 12" by 12".

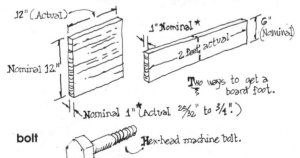

12" (Actual)

Nominal 12."

1" Nominal *

2 feet actual

6" (Nominal)

Two ways to get a board foot.

Nominal 1" (Actual 25/32" to 3/4".)

bolt

Hex-head machine bolt.

butt joint
The simplest method of joining two pieces of wood—the end, or edge, of one piece against the side of the other.

Butt Joint.

cabinet-grade hardwood
A grade commonly applied to **FAS** (Firsts and Seconds) hardwood that has been carefully seasoned and/or **kiln-dried** to a moisture content of five to nine percent.

cabinet making
The fine craft of making all kinds of furniture from wood. Distinguished from carpentry, which generally uses coarser tools and tolerances.

carpentry
See **cabinetmaking.**

cedar
A **softwood** lumber that comes from any of several evergreen trees of the genus *Cedrus.* Naturally resistant to rot and insects.

Celotex
See insulation board.

clear
In lumber, the absence of any knots or other defects.

common
Lumber with defects. Suitable for utility shelving or construction that is to be hidden. In **redwood** and **cedar** this grade can look rustic and quite handsome. See below and also **grade.**

#1 common
Highest **common** grade. It is lesser in quality than **grade D select.** Characterized by sound, tight knots.

#2 common
Lesser than **#1 common**—sound knots that can be sealed. Used for siding, shelving, paneling.

#3 common Lesser than **#2 common**—building strength; suitable for use in fences, boxes. A good choice for the crate boxes described on p. 147.

#4 common You guessed it: lesser than **#3 common**—used for general construction that is to be hidden—subfloors, sheathing, etc.

corner iron

corrugated fastener Used in making light-duty **miter** joints.

cup Tendency of **milled** lumber to curve in the direction of the grain.

(cupped board)

cup hook

cutting, and cutting a line Painter's jargon for making a straight line along a wall and ceiling joint, along a window **mullion,** or simply to separate two colors on a single surface. With practice you can do it with a brush. I recommend a pad painter (p. 27).

dado A wide groove cut by hand or with a **dado** blade.

dado blade.

dado

double hung A classic window design incorporating an upper, outside sash that slides down, and a lower, inside sash that slides up. See also p. 78.

dowel A round wooden rod available in diameters from ⅛" to 1½". The 1½" size is often sold under the name **closet pole.** See also **molding.**

drywall A plasterlike material formed into sheets, usually 4' by 8', and covered with paper. Since around the 1940s this has been the most common material used for interior wall paneling. Joints are finished with tape and spackle to make a continuous wall surface. It replaced wet plaster—hence: "dry" wall. Also goes by the names **plasterboard, gypsum board, Sheetrock,** and **wallboard.**

eyebolt

FAS First and Seconds. The highest grade of hardwood sold for **cabinetmaking.**

fiber-glass strapping tape An adhesive tape incorporating fibers of glass to make it exceptionally strong in **tension.**

flake board See **particle board.**

frame and panel A traditional method of constructing doors and the sides of cabinets and chests.

frame

panel

G 1 S Good one side. Quality rating for lumber.

grade Quality rating for lumber, as in "grade B and better." (See below and also **common.**)

grade B and better Highest grade of lumber—many pieces **clear** (free of knots).

grade C select Lesser grade than **B and better**—still fine enough for cabinet work and trim.

grade D select Lesser than **grade C select**—clear on one side, small defects on the other. The next lowest grade is **#1 common.**

gusset The diagonal brace on an **angle iron** which gives it resistance to **racking.** Also any triangular piece serving the same function. See also **racking.**

Gusset

gypsum board See **drywall.**

hardwood Wood from broad-leaved flowering trees, distinguished from wood of a conifer. See also **softwood.**

hardboard A somewhat ambiguous term for composition boards. Probably it most often refers to **Masonite.**

hollow-core door The current rage in interior doors (because they're cheap). The perimeter is solid wood, the inside is an "egg-crate" of thin plywood, or even cardboard. The front and back surfaces are ⅛" plywood veneer. They make better tables than doors.

Cutaway view of hollow-core door

hollow-wall anchors Fasteners made especially for **hollow-core doors** and paneled walls. See also pp. 41–43.

insulation board The generic name for a soft composition board made of cellulose fibers. Usually sold in 4' by 8' sheets, ½" thick, and more commonly called by trade names including *Celotex, Homosote,* and whatever your dealer calls it.

joist Wooden beams, usually 2" by 6", 2" by 8", 2" by 10", etc. Used to hold up a ceiling and the floor above.

kick-plate A protective molding, usually recessed, at the base of a cabinet, stove, or refrigerator. It is often dark-colored so as not to show kick marks.

Cabinet   Toe space
Kick-plate

kiln-dried Designation for lumber that has been dried in temperature-controlled ovens (kilns). Compared with **AD,** (air-dried).

lag eyebolt

latex-based paint Paint made of **latex,** a synthetic rubber (the vehicle), water (the **thinner**), and pigment (the coloring material). See also p. 26.

lath A wood or metal grid used as the substrate for wet plaster.

"Keying" effect of plaster on lath.

Lath has many other uses. It is the basis for **lath** houses and trellises. It also makes an interesting interior wall covering. (See p. 23.) Lath is usually rough-sawn from **redwood** or **cedar.** It's ¼" to ⅜" thick, and about 1⅜" wide. It's sold in 50 piece bundles of 4', 6', or 8' lengths, or sometimes by the individual stick.

ledger A horizontal board attached to several vertical posts. It distributes the load of any weight put on it to all the posts, evenly. Also see p. 40.

level A tool used to determine true horizontal or true vertical. Also the condition of being truly horizontal.

light Architect's parlance for the glass panes of a window.

A five-light double hung window

Masonite A trade name for a dense, dark-colored board usually sold in 4' by 8' sheets in thicknesses of ⅛" or ¼". It is available in two densities: *tempered*—dark brown, heavy, hard on saw blades, but can be scored (cut partway through with a sharp knife) and then snapped in two; and *untempered*—light brown, lighter in weight; can be cut cleanly with several passes of a **mat knife.**

mat knife A tool designed for cutting thick cardboard (mats). Extra, reversible blades are stored in the two-piece handle. Use sharp blades for safety.

Mat knife and blades

mending plate

182

milled Lumber that has been smooth-surfaced in a power planer or with a hand plane. **Nominal** dimensions are based on **milled** (or finished) sizes of lumber.

miter and miter box A right-angle joint made by cutting two pieces of wood at 45° angles. To make such a joint you **"miter"** it with a **miter box.**

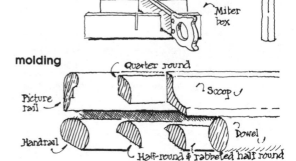

Miter
Miter box

molding

Quarter round
Scoop
Picture rail
Handrail
Dowel
Half-round & rabbeted half round

Molly A patented fastener used with hollow walls or doors. See also p. 42.

mullion A vertical strip dividing the panes of a window. See also **muntin.**

muntin A horizontal strip dividing the panes of a window.

nails

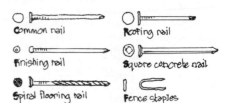

Common nail
Roofing nail
Finishing nail
Square concrete nail
Spiral flooring nail
Fence staples

nailing strip A strip of wood installed like a **ledger** to bolster up a shelf or ledge.

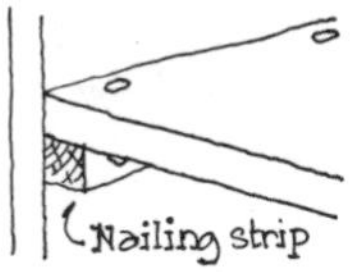

Nailing strip

Can also be used with screws, of course.

nominal dimension
The common size-designation for lumber. It is based on the **rough-cut** size of the lumber.

Nominal (Rough-cut) Size (inches)	Actual Size (inches)	Nominal (Rough-cut) Size (inches)	Actual Size (inches)
1 × 2	¾ × 1½	2 × 4	1½ × 3½
1 × 3	¾ × 2½	2 × 6	1½ × 5½
1 × 4	¾ × 3½	2 × 8	1½ × 7¼
1 × 6	¾ × 5½	2 × 10	1½ × 9¼
1 × 8	¾ × 7¼	2 × 12	1½ × 11¼
1 × 10	¾ × 9¼	4 × 4	3½ × 3½
1 × 12	¾ × 11¼	4 × 6	3½ × 5½

nut

Square nut   Cap nut   Wing nut   Hex nut   Knurled nut

oil-based paint
Paint made of oil (the vehicle), pigment (the coloring material), and mineral spirits (the **solvent**). Fumes are volatile and toxic. May soon be illegal to manufacture because of environmental considerations. See p. 26.

particle board
A composition board made from wood chips or flakes bonded in a mixture of sawdust and a plastic bonding agent. Usually sold in 4′ by 8′ sheets in thicknesses from ⅜″ to ¾″. Also called **flake board.**

peg
A short dowel—often with screwlike threads—used to fasten boards, especially edge to edge.

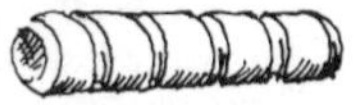

penny
A rating for nails, originally the price per hundred—now used as a measure of length.

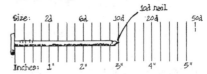

Size: 2d   6d   10d   10d nail   20d   50d

Inches: 1″   2″   3″   4″   5″

The symbol for penny is *d* (from *denarius,* an early Roman coin). Since shank diameter increases with length, the penny rating has come to stand for size and weight.

pilot hole
A preliminary, smaller hole drilled—sometimes with a special bit—to make driving a screw or nail easier, neater, and/or less likely to split a narrow piece of wood.

pine
A **softwood** lumber. The kind of pine lumber available varies with the locale; in the West it's usually ponderosa pine; in the East, white pine; and in the South, yellow pine. Confusingly, ponderosa is also sometimes called "yellow pine."

plaster
A cementlike material that is mixed with water and applied over wood or metal **lath.**

plaster board
See **drywall.**

plumb bob
A tool made to be hung on a string—used like a compass to indicate a true vertical line. See also **level.**

polyurethane varnish and foam
A plastic material used to make a hard varnish and also expanded into polyurethane foam. The latter is extensively used in mattresses and cushions, either in block form or shredded. Toxic fumes are released

in manufacture and (perhaps) residually. Polyurethane foam will also burn, contrary to original industry claims.

R. W. L.   Random width and lengths (of lumber).

racking   The tendency of any frame structure fastened at four corners to become a parallelogram. Prevented by diagonal bracing or angle brackets.

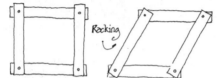

redwood   A **softwood** lumber that comes from either of two giant West Coast evergreen trees, genus *Sequoia sempervirens* ("redwood") or *Sequoia gigantea* (giant Sequoia). Naturally resistant to decay.

rough-sawn or rough-cut   Lumber fresh from the sawmill where it was converted from logs. Dimensions of lumber are based on the **rough-cut** size.

"S" hook

S 2 S   Surfaced two sides. Lumber which has been **rough-cut,** then **milled** on two sides, usually the faces.

S 1 S   Surfaced one side. Lumber which has been **rough-cut,** then **milled** on one side, usually one of the faces.

S 1 E   Surfaced one edge. Lumber which has been **rough-cut,** then **milled** on one edge.

screw eye

screw hook

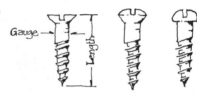

screw pilot   See **pilot hole.**

screws

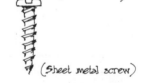

Flat head   Oval head   Round head
(Wood screws)

(Sheet metal screw)

select   Lumber of good appearance and finishing quality.

Sheetrock®   See **drywall.**

shellac   A clear finishing material made by dissolving the resinous substance (secreted by the Asian lac insect) in alcohol. Not as durable as varnish, but healthier to use.

Shoulder hook

socket wrench   A tool with a handle and changeable sockets in metric or English sizes to fit hexagonal bolts, nuts, and lag screws. See p. 40.

softwood   Generally refers to lumber from cone-bearing trees. Including **redwood, pine, cedar.** Compare **hardwood.**

solvent Any liquid which dissolves (or thins) a solid, plastic, or liquid material. Usually volatile and flammable. Alcohol is a solvent for shellac. Turpentine or mineral spirits is a solvent for **varnish** and **oil-based paints.** Water is a solvent for **latex-based paints.**

special fittings

Leg plate

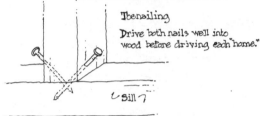

Corner brace

Corner table plate

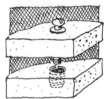

Threaded insert

standard A grade of lumber. Usually applied to **softwoods.**

stud You may have your definition, but to a carpenter this means a regularly spaced vertical member (usually 2" by 4") in a wall. See p. 38.

T-plate

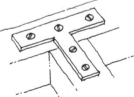

tension or tensile strength A pulling force, or the resistance to a pulling force, acting along the length of a construction member.

thinner See **solvent.**

toenail A strong, but somewhat crude, method of fastening a **butt joint.** Used for nailing studs to sill and plate in stud-wall construction.

Toenailing

Drive both nails well into wood before driving each "home."

sill

toggle bolt or Toggler A special fastener used with hollow walls. See p. 43.

turnbuckle

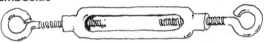

utility A lumber grade. Usually applied to **softwoods** used in construction. See also **standard. Utility** is better than **standard;** both are surfaced on four sides.

varnish A clear, hard, finishing material made from resin dissolved in oil and mineral spirits. When dry, it is resistant to alcohol, water, and detergents. It will darken wood somewhat and also tends to give it a yellowish color, especially with age.

warp Twisting of wood caused by improper drying and/or excessive moisture.

washer

185

Last Words

The Moveable Nest Update
is a two-to four-page, 8 ½ by
14 inch newspaper. It will
give you the latest revelations
on my moveable nest, current
news, and views on the landlord-
tenant front, product reviews
and previews of material from
The Moveable Nest II. In addition,
you'll be joining a network
of readers like yourself.
By sharing our experiential
wealth we can all get better
at this.

Write to:

Tom Schneider
P.O. Box 23
San Anselmo, California
94960

Index